D1569173

The Operas of Gian Carlo Menotti, 1937-1972:

A Selective Bibliography

by
LYNDAL GRIEB

The Scarecrow Press, Inc.
Metuchen, N.J.   1974

Library of Congress Cataloging in Publication Data

Grieb, Lyndal, 1940-
    The operas of Gian Carlo Menotti, 1937-1972.

    1. Menotti, Gian Carlo, 1911-   --Bibliography.
I. Title.
ML134.M533G7   016.7821'092'4   74-16310
ISBN 0-8108-0743-2

To Greg

TABLE OF CONTENTS

Introduction   v

Biographical Sketch   vii

Bibliographical Essay   xii

A SELECTIVE BIO-BIBLIOGRAPHY

I.   Works by Menotti   17

         The Operas   17
         The Scores   18
         Librettos   19
         Recordings   20
         Opera Selections   21
         Book Adaptations   22

II.   Works About Menotti   23

III. General Reference Works   25

IV.   Periodical Articles (by Opera)   40

V.   General Periodical Articles   117

VI.   Newspaper Articles (by Opera)   137

VII. General Newspaper Articles   177

Index   183

INTRODUCTION

The writer hopes that this bio-bibliography on Menotti will be a permanently useful research guide for the lay reader and the scholar. No attempt has been made to include all found materials; rather the aim has been to exclude certain announcements of the composer's plans and other materials that are neither reviews, analyses or commentaries, articles written by Menotti, nor biographical matter. Very brief reviews are present because they are an important part of an opera's performance history.

Predictably many of the periodical and newspaper articles are cited in Music Index. Other index sources are: Reader's Guide to Periodical Literature, Guide to the Performing Arts, Education Index, Social Sciences and Humanities Index, British Humanities Index, Biography Index, Dramatic Index and Annual Magazine Subject Index. Still other helpful research guides are: National Union Catalog; Library of Congress Catalog. Books: Subjects-; Library of Congress Catalog. Music and Phonorecords; and the New York Public Library. Reference Department. Dictionary Catalog of the Music Collection.

Books listed in "General Reference" reflect mainly the collections in the Kansas City (Missouri) Public Library's Art and Music Department, the Conservatory of Music Library at the University of Missouri at Kansas City, and the Music Library at Memphis State University, Tennessee. No effort was made to assure complete coverage in this section. Many of these materials are useful chiefly for compact biographical sketches while a few are more suitable for the serious student.

The notes on photographs and illustrations are intended to provide a record for community groups, opera workshops and other organizations for the location of pictorial aids.

The "See Also" references should aid in finding occasions when two Menotti operas were performed together as a double bill. This has often been the case with The Telephone and The Medium.

Although neither The Unicorn nor The Death of The Bishop of Brindisi qualify as operas for this writer, they are included as a convenience for the user. They illustrate the versatility of Menotti's work.

Grateful acknowledgment goes to Naomi Jolly, Tomas Figueroa, Constance Barrett and Madeleine Jappe for their translations. Barbara Wylie has been the able typist of the manuscript. The writer has written paraphrases of the translations. The enthusiasm of Virginia Algermissen, a true lover of opera and the writer's research advisor at the University of Missouri, has been greatly encouraging.

BIOGRAPHICAL SKETCH

Gian Carlo Menotti was born July 7, 1911, in Cadegliano, Italy, to a large prosperous family. In his adolescence he was taken to Milan where he attended the Milan Conservatory between 1923 and 1928. In Milan he composed his first opera and libretto, The Death of Pierrot, in which everyone dies. Its importance seems to be solely that it was Menotti's first opera composition. Unfortunately, in Milan he became a spoiled favorite of society matrons, causing his mother to feel that his remaining there could only harm him. She sent him to the United States for musical discipline at the Curtis Institute of Music in Philadelphia.

He was introduced to American audiences with an "opera buffa," Amelia Goes to the Ball, first performed at the Philadelphia Academy of Music on April 1, 1937. Contrary to his later practice, he wrote the libretto first in Italian. The performance benefitted from having Fritz Reiner as its conductor and critics were generous in their praise of the work, mentioning its charm and skillful use of stock characters.

The Old Maid and the Thief was, again, opera buffa in genre, but was initially a radio opera commissioned by NBC Radio, the first of its kind. In later years it becomes an amusing companion for more serious opera like The Medium.

In the early Forties the young composer experienced his only real failure, The Island God, produced at the Metropolitan Opera. Menotti later admitted that the philosophical theme makes for a weak opera. The Island God has become a historical curiosity mainly because it died for lack of performance.

Apparently the pronounced failure of this work was a turning point, for The Medium marked a radical departure in starkness and contemporary atmosphere. Its treatment of reality and fantasy foreshadowed one of the composer's primary concerns. The title role, Mme. Flora, became one of the greatest roles in contemporary music drama. Winthrop Sargeant ranks The Medium as a masterpiece along with the later Consul and Amahl. Certainly The Medium has become a mainstay in the United States.

"The Telephone," a frothy one-acter, made an excellent curtain raiser for the darker Medium. There are only two characters, Lucy and Ben, plus the telephone, the most important prop. Menotti's versatility with the commonplace again manifests itself.

The Consul represented his first effort at a larger, longer work. This dark drama of bureaucratic indifference to the suffering individual struck fire on Broadway for a long run--then unheard of for contemporary opera. Patricia Neway built her career from the tragic Magda Sorel, symbolic of the displaced person after World War II. Menotti introduced a new potent realism with this work, which won him a Pulitzer Prize.

Television history occurred December 24, 1951, with the transmission of the first opera commissioned for television, Amahl and The Night Visitors on NBC-TV. Toscanini was touched by Amahl's lyrical simplicity and universality; his judgment proved accurate since the tale of the crippled Amahl and his sacrifice of his crutch to the Magi has become a Christmas classic. Even small community groups have found it unusually adaptable for production. To the lay public, Amahl is Menotti more than any other opera.

One of Menotti's strongest preoccupations has been the conflict between faith and skepticism. In The Saint of Bleecker Street the representative of faith is Annina while her brother Michele is the skeptic. Although The Saint won another Pulitzer Prize and ran on Broadway, it was not a large success. The heavy emphasis on religious piety (e.g., the stigmata experience) apparently offended many. The Saint qualifies as "grand opera" with three acts and impressive, large scaled choral writing.

The Unicorn, The Gorgon and The Manticore was first given at the chamber music festival in the Library of Congress. Such an offbeat work probably will never attract a large audience although many have admired the use of the madrigal form and the original treatment of dance, chorus and orchestra. Like the unconventional Poet, it may always puzzle the lay audience.

Maria Golovin premiered August 20, 1958, in Brussels, to a lukewarm reception. The male central figure, the blind Donato, failed to arouse necessary sympathy. A revised version may yet prove more successful.

For his next work Menotti turned again to the television medium for "Labyrinth," a one-act "riddle." This work exploited photographic effects that would be impossible on the stage. Some critics have stated that the music and libretto are far from Menotti's best.

The Death of the Bishop of Brindisi, a cantata,
premiered May 18, 1963, at the May Festival in Cincinnati,
to an enthusiastic audience. The story is that of a bishop
who berates himself for having permitted the Children's
Crusade with its mass slaughter of the innocent. An attempt to produce this work as an opera has not yet been
realized successfully.

Later in the same year, 1963, the Opéra Comique in
Paris became the theatre for the premiere of The Last
Savage, a sarcastic comic opera that French critics generally roasted. Some United States critics were more generous with praise for the Metropolitan Opera production and
the work. Menotti here attempted a departure from contemporary operatic writing.

"Martin's Lie" premiered at the Bath Festival in 1964
before a moved audience in the Bristol Cathedral. Several
critics were troubled by the morality of the short work in
which a boy's lie is caused by his need for a father.

Contemporary ideas such as invaders from space and
electronic music get an amusing treatment in "Help! Help!
The Globolinks," which was first given in German at Hamburg in 1968. Critics noted the "mixed-media" sound and
look to this opera, for the choreography and settings generally impress more than the music. Menotti has said the
opera is for the young and the young at heart.

Fighting a deadline for the New York City Opera,
Menotti rushed to complete The Most Important Man in the
spring of 1971, his first commentary on racial prejudice.
Although the locale is not specified, there are hints of
South Africa's apartheid. Irving Kolodin found it very forgettable while Winthrop Sargeant called the new work impressive.

In general Menotti is classed as a conservative, traditional composer who is not in the serial, atonal school, although, to give one exception, he uses such music in fun in The Last Savage. Many have alluded to his sentimentality and melodramatic situations while conceding that The Medium, Amahl and The Consul are probably permanent repertoire in American opera.

BIBLIOGRAPHICAL ESSAY

A survey of this bibliography indicates that most of the literature on Menotti comes from either periodicals or newspapers and consists largely of reviews of performances. A second much smaller group comprises critical commentaries and analyses that examine a particular opera or operas (with or without reference to a given performance), or articles that reveal Menotti's philosophy and operatic creeds, or biographical pieces. Many of the books in the "General Reference" section combine a biographical sketch with criticism of various operas. Noticeable exceptions to this pattern are the Tricoire study, however lacking in analytical depth it is, and the dissertations.

Reviews of the operas vary greatly from a brief paragraph, a mere mention of a performance, to analysis within a review. Even brief reviews aid in a running chronology of a work's performance history though they otherwise seem valueless to the scholar. Whether minuscule or sizeable these reviews have certain similarities in content.

One believes a valid review should reveal the audience's reaction to the opera. A critic may be largely negative about a new work while the audience showed approval. In Menotti's career several works have elicited such differing responses from critics and the public. As an example, The Last Savage probably fared better with audiences at the

Metropolitan Opera than with certain critics. In fairness, most reviewers do report the audience reaction.

Plot summaries tend to be no longer than two paragraphs. The usual rule is a capsule form of the essential facts of the action; much rarer is a plot rendering with detail and explanations of character motivation. One will find more detailed plot summaries in some of the general reference materials.

In the reviews, Menotti's music tends to get a brief description as to the general impression. Much has been written about the "derivative" and "eclectic" nature of his music; critics claim he is influenced by Puccini, Stravinsky, Mussorgsky and others--usually without providing evidence of the influence. The basis for such statements is obviously Menotti's sound.

In discussing The Medium, The Consul and The Saint in particular, writers have often turned to Menotti's tendency toward melodrama. To some he is an exponent of the Grand Guignol school of shock. There is the mysterious hand on Mme. Flora's throat and her shooting of Toby in The Medium, the dream death-dance in The Consul and the killing of Desideria in The Saint. Some critics have called such sensational events "vulgar" while others see dramatic validity in their use. This debate shows no signs of resolution.

One naturally expects in an opera review a criticism of the singing and acting. Very early critics realized that since the composer is his own stage director and librettist, his works would be much more than singing straight out to the house--that he sought performers who could sacrifice beautiful tone and arias to create characters. For this reason one finds acting in a Menotti performance of equal importance with singing and the reviews tend to reflect this reality. A Magda, Mme. Flora, Annina or Magician require that the singer strike an equal integration between his acting and singing; to deemphasize either is to damage the role seriously.

The problem with many reviews is the writer's failure to mention all of the cast. In Menotti more than in 19th-Century opera, the minor roles are an indivisible part of the dramatic whole. In The Saint all of the minor characters are valid types of people in "Little Italy." So in the music drama their efforts are important and should be reviewed.

As expected, many reviewers mention also the sets, conducting, and the production's general impact. In Maria Golovin the original sets were a key to the work's symbolism. The critic would be remiss not to discuss the designer's apparent intentions.

Both the reviews and analytical articles would be stronger if musical quotations were used with greater frequency. The present work includes only a few examples of articles with musical examples. To mention two, there are Charles Stuart's "Menotti and Mr. Smith" on The Consul (in Halle) and R. F. Deke's notes on The Medium (in Film Music Notes). Such quotations give concrete evidence that the reviewer has examined the score; this can indicate the use of a more objective yardstick for evaluation than would be a mere hearing.

Although generally the literature needs more depth and perception in considering the recurring themes of Menotti, they have fortunately not wholly been neglected. There are,

for example, the pairs of opposites--faith and disbelief, and
reality and fantasy. Only a few have noted the contrast between Menotti's strong feminine characters and his weak
male leads. Many writers have commented, however, on
his musical contrasts and methods of placing tension and
lightness near one another.

The writer cites the following articles as illustrating
the sort of commentary and analysis that strengthen critical
writing in a desirable way. Winthrop Sargeant's "Orlando
in Mount Kisco" in the New Yorker is excellent for combining biography, commentary on the operas and a sensitive
understanding of the man. John Mason Brown shows the in-
sights a drama critic can bring to opera as theater in the
Saturday Review, in his review of The Medium and "The
Telephone." Felix Aprahamian's review of The Consul in
the World Review is exceptional for its grasp of the work's
contrasts. For a discussion of the operas as music dramas,
one is referred to Meredith Lillich's article in the Educational Theatre Journal.

Most of the periodical and newspaper articles that
are not reviews or general commentary have been included
because they give the composer's artistic attitudes toward
opera and theater and opera as theater. They also are quite
useful for revealing the composer's intentions in his operas.
And we learn about his inspirations from him. The New
York Times article, "Notes on Opera as Basic Theatre, "
is an apt illustration of the usefulness of this type of material.

Casmus' dissertation is invaluable because it remains
at this writing the only in-depth study in English. Since her
work earned her a Ph. D. in speech and theater the slant is

not that of a musician's. Today its greatest limitations are
a total absence of musical quotations, discussion of these,
and the exclusion of operas written after The Saint. One
hopes for an equally masterly study on later libretti and
dramatic techniques plus the musical quotations.

Tricoire's book is important on a simpler level.
One has found no other studies, apart from the dissertations and limited articles in general reference books. Tricoire is most useful for his handy synopses through The
Last Savage and the section, "Menotti and the Critic." The
biggest disappointment in his book is the lack of probing
analysis.

The later operas after The Saint are especially open
for extensive dissection. Because Menotti is still strongly
circulating, these studies are almost inevitable for the future.

A SELECTIVE BIO-BIBLIOGRAPHY

I. WORKS BY MENOTTI

The Operas

AMAHL AND THE NIGHT VISITORS. Opera in one act.
    Libretto by the composer. First performance: NBC
    Television, December 24, 1951.

AMELIA GOES TO THE BALL [Amelia al Ballo]. Comic
    opera in one act. Libretto by the composer. First
    performance: Academy of Music, Philadelphia, April
    1, 1937.

THE CONSUL. Opera in three acts. Libretto by the com-
    poser. First performance: New York City, March
    15, 1950.

THE DEATH OF THE BISHOP OF BRINDISI. Dramatic
    cantata. Libretto by the composer. First performance:
    Cincinnati, Ohio, May 18, 1963.

HELP! HELP! THE GLOBOLINKS [Hilfe! Hilfe! Die Glo-
    bolinks]. Opera in one act. Libretto by the composer.
    First performance: Hamburg State Opera, December 2,
    1968.

THE ISLAND GOD. Opera in two acts. Libretto by the
    composer. First performance: Metropolitan Opera,
    February 20, 1942.

LABYRINTH. Television opera in one act. Libretto by the
    composer. First performance: NBC Television,
    March 5, 1963.

THE LAST SAVAGE [Le Dernier Sauvage]. Comic opera in
    three acts. Libretto by the composer. First per-
    formance: Opera Comique, Paris, October 22, 1963.

MARIA GOLOVIN. Opera in three acts. Libretto by the
    composer. First performance: Brussels, August 20,
    1958.

MARTIN'S LIE. Opera in one act. Libretto by the com-
    poser. First performance: Bristol Cathedral, England,
    June 3, 1964.

THE MEDIUM. Opera in two acts. Libretto by the com-
    poser. First performance: Columbia University, New
    York City, May 8, 1946.

THE MOST IMPORTANT MAN. Opera in three acts. Li-
    bretto by the composer. First performance: New
    York City Opera, March 7, 1971.

THE OLD MAID AND THE THIEF. Comic opera in one act.
    Libretto by the composer. First radio performance:
    NBC Radio, April 22, 1939; first stage performance:
    Philadelphia Opera Company, February 11, 1941.

THE SAINT OF BLEECKER STREET. Opera in three acts.
    Libretto by the composer. First performance: Broad-
    way Theatre, New York City, December 27, 1954.

THE TELEPHONE. Comic opera in one act. Libretto by
    the composer. First performance: Heckscher Theater,
    New York City, February 18, 1947.

THE UNICORN, THE GORGON AND THE MANTICORE.
    Madrigal fable for small orchestra, chorus and dancers.
    First performance: Library of Congress, Washington,
    D. C., October 21, 1956.

The Scores

AMAHL AND THE NIGHT VISITORS. New York: G. Schir-
    mer, 1951. 36 pp.

AMELIA AL BALLO. Trans. George Mead. Milan: G.
    Ricordi, 1952. 166 pp.
        English and Italian. Ten page prelude.

AMELIA GEHT ZUM BALL. Trans. Georg C. Winkler.
    New York: G. Ricordi, 1939. 42 pp.

THE CONSUL. New York: G. Schirmer, 1950. 291 pp.
Cast given for the first New York production.

HELP! HELP! THE GLOBOLINKS. Trans. Kurt Honolka.
New York: G. Schirmer, 1969. 112 pp.
English and German.

THE MEDIUM. French version by Leon Kochnitzky. New
York: G. Schirmer, 1947. 115 pp.
Cast given for the first performance at Columbia
University. Revised edition in 1968.

THE MEDIUM. n.p., 194-? 2 v.
Score and libretto. "Black-line print from manuscript copy, with Norwegian translation written in,
in ink." (Library of Congress Catalog. Music
and Phono-records).

THE OLD MAID AND THE THIEF. New York: G. Ricordi,
1943. 183 pp.
Twelve page overture. Includes announcements
before the scenes for radio production. Later
edition in 1954.

THE SAINT OF BLEECKER STREET. New York: G.
Schirmer, 1954. 307 pp.
Revised edition in 1969.

THE TELEPHONE. n.p. 194-?
Score and libretto. "Black-line print from manuscript copy, with Norwegian translation written in,
in ink." (Library of Congress Catalog. Music
and Phono-records).

THE UNICORN, THE GORGON AND THE MANTICORE.
New York: G. Ricordi, 1957. 156 pp.
English. The original orchestration calls for flute,
oboe, clarinet, bassoon, trumpet, violoncello,
double-bass, percussion and harp.

Librettos

AMAHL AND THE NIGHT VISITORS. New York: G.
Schirmer, 1951. 36 pp.

AMELIA GOES TO THE BALL [Amelia al Ballo]. English

version by George Mead. New York: G. Ricordi,
1938. 37 pp.

THE CONSUL. New York: G. Schirmer, 1950. 56 pp.

THE ISLAND GOD. English version by Fleming McLiesh.
New York: G. Ricordi, 1942. 30 pp.

THE LAST SAVAGE [L'Ultimo Selvaggio]. English version
by George Mead. New York: Franco Colombo, 1963.
48 pp.

MARIA GOLOVIN. New York: G. Ricordi, 1959. 61 pp.

THE SAINT OF BLEECKER STREET. New York: Radio
Corporation of America, 1954. 54 pp.

Recordings

AMAHL AND THE NIGHT VISITORS. King, Yaghjian, Mc-
Collum, Patterson, Cross. Grossman, cond. RCA
Victor LM 2762, LSC 2862.
1964 recording. Cast of the NBC Opera Company
television production, December, 1963. Libretto
and notes.

_____. Kuhlman, Allen, McKinley, Lishner, Aiken,
Monachino. Schippers, cond. RCA Victor 1512.
Original cast of the 1951 NBC telecast. Pro-
gram notes by Menotti.

Highlights from AMAHL AND THE NIGHT VISITORS.
Soloists and chorus. Schippers, cond. RCA Victor
ERA 120.
Original cast of NBC television production.

AMELIA AL BALLO. Carosio, Panerai, Prandelli, Amadini,
Campi, Zanolli, Mazzoni. Sanzogno, cond. Angel 35140.
Photos: La Scala premiere in 1954 with the same
cast and the Metropolitan Opera 1938 production
with Amelia (Muriel Dickson) and Chief of Police
(Norman Gordon). Libretto.

THE CONSUL. Powers, Neway. Engel, cond. Decca
DXA 101, DL 9500-9501
Original cast. Notes by Menotti and Louis Unter-
meyer. Libretto.

THE DEATH OF THE BISHOP OF BRINDISI. Chookasian,
London. New England Conservatory Chorus, Catholic
Memorial and St. Joseph's High School Glee Clubs.
Leinsdorf, cond. RCA Victor LM LSC 2785.
1965 recording. Libretto.

MARIA GOLOVIN. Duval, Las, Neway, Handt, Chapman,
Cross, Adler, cond. 3 RCA Victor LM 6142
1958 recording. Notes by Samuel Chotzinoff.
Libretto.

THE MEDIUM. Resnik, Blegen, Derr, Patrick, Carlson.
Mester, cond. Columbia MS 7386.
1970 recording. Notes by Menotti include an excellent plot summary.

_____. Keller, Powers, Dame, Mastice, Rogier. Bala-
ban, cond. 2 Columbia OL 4174-4175, OSL 154
(Paired with THE TELEPHONE).
Notes by Goddard Lieberson. Libretto.

THE OLD MAID AND THE THIEF. Blegen, M. Baker,
Reynolds, Reardon. Mester, cond. Mercury 90521.
Notes by Menotti and James Lyons. Libretto.

THE SAINT OF BLEECKER STREET. Ruggiero, Poleri,
Lane, Lishner. Schippers, cond. 2 RCA Victor LM
6032-6033.
Libretto.

THE TELEPHONE. Cotlow, Rogier, Balaban, cond. 2 Columbia OL 4174-4175, OSL 154 (Paired with THE
MEDIUM).
1949 recording. Notes by Goddard Lieberson.
Libretto.

THE UNICORN, THE GORGON AND THE MANTICORE.
Schippers, cond. Angel 35437.
1957 recording. Program notes and libretto by
Menotti.

Opera Selections

AMAHL AND THE NIGHT VISITORS. Selections. New York:
G. Schirmer, 1952. "Introduction, March and Shep-
herd's Dance." 21 pp.

THE CONSUL. "The Empty-Handed Traveler. " New York:
    G. Schirmer, 1950.
        Range is low A to high F sharp.   5 pp.

_____. "The Lullaby. " New York: G. Schirmer, 1950.
    Piano reduction by Thomas Schippers.
        Range is low A to high E flat.   5 pp.

_____. "To this we've come. " New York: G. Schirmer,
    1950. Aria for high voice and piano.   Piano reduction
    by Thomas Schippers.   18 pp.
        Magda's aria with a range from low B to high A
        flat.

THE MEDIUM. "The Black Swan. " New York: G. Schir-
    mer, 1947.   French version by Leon Kochnitzky.
        Range is low D to high G.   7 pp.

Book Adaptations

AMAHL AND THE NIGHT VISITORS.   New York: Whittlesey
    House (division of McGraw-Hill), 1952.   Narrative
    adaptation by Frances Frost.   Illustrated by Roger
    Duvoisin.
        The exact dialogue is used.   Useful introduction
        for young readers.

HELP! HELP! THE GLOBOLINKS!   New York: McGraw-
    Hill, 1970.   Adapted by Leigh Dean from the original
    libretto.   Illustrated by Milton Glaser.
        Musical quotations are from the prelude, the vocal
        parts for Dr. Stone, Timothy and Emily and the
        score for the electrical music.   Delightful illustra-
        tions in mod style.

THE LAST SAVAGE.   Greenwich, Connecticut: New York
    Graphic Society in co-operation with the Metropolitan
    Opera Guild, 1964.   Drawing by Beni Montresor.
        Montresor's settings are used in the Metropolitan
        Opera production.   Quarto size.

II. WORKS ABOUT MENOTTI

Casmus, Mary Irene. Gian-Carlo Menotti: His Dramatic
Techniques: A Study Based on Works Written 1937-
1954. (Doctoral dissertation.) New York: Columbia
University, 1962.
Masterly study of the composer's dramatic techniques and principles he uses in writing librettos.
The operas run through THE SAINT. Casmus or-
ganizes the libretto by the media the operas are
intended for--i. e., traditional opera house, theatre,
radio and television. She finds a number of criteria to help her analysis of plot, characterization,
language and theatrical concept. The latter is de-
fined as "the author's idea of the visual details of
action, characterization and setting" (page 39).
Since the dissertation is in speech and theater it is
not surprising to note that the criteria includes the
intelligibility and singability of the text and theatrical sense. Casmus describes the exposition,
rising action and climax of each plot as she relates
each to a play's structure. Menotti's great emphasis is on telling a story. Casmus lists his most
consistent ways of storytelling such as well-defined
characters, whether individualized or typed. Her
conclusions on his libretto's characteristics are
very valuable. She rates him highest on theatrical
sense, lowest on literary quality and continuity of
action. Casmus concludes that Menotti gifts are
best suited to short, intimate operas that are small
scaled. With review excerpts, many textual quotations and bibliography.

Holden, Randall LeConte, Jr. Part I: The Seattle Production
of The Telephone by Gian Carlo Menotti. (Doctoral
dissertation.) Seattle: University of Washington, 1970.
"I: The first part of this dissertation documents a
production of Gian Carlo Menotti's short, sophisti-
cated opera, THE TELEPHONE, which was pre-

pared under the author's direction.   Although biographical material on Menotti, a short summation
of musical style, and a catalogue of his operas are
included, the focus is on the stage direction of this
comic opera: its characters, directorial problems
and solutions, set and costume design, and lighting. " (Dissertation Abstracts: September-October,
1971, 1551-A).

Tricoire, Robert.   Gian-Carlo Menotti: L'Homme et son
    Oeuvre....   Paris: Seghers, 1966.
        Important critical work that discusses the operas
        from THE DEATH OF PIERROT to THE LAST
        SAVAGE.   With dialogue excerpts in French and
        English, many excerpts from reviews and a sec-
        tion, "Menotti and the Critic. "   Scenes and musical
        forms (duet, aria, etc.) are indicated.   Synopsis
        of the operas.   "Menotti and the Critic" has crit-
        ical excerpts by Winthrop Sargeant in New Yorker,
        Henry Butler in Opera News, Rene Dumesnil in
        Le Monde, Robert Horan, Robert Kemp in France
        Illustrated, Giorgio Vigolo in Il Mondo, Marcel
        Landowski, Daniel Lesur, Henri Sauguet, Andre
        Boll and Marcel Delannoy.   With a discography.
        Photos: Marine Powers as Mme. Flora in THE
        MEDIUM, Patricia Neway as Magda in THE CON-
        SUL, Menotti directing a boy as Amahl, Menotti as
        a child and as a student at the Curtis Institute of
        Music with Samuel Barber, Menotti with Ionesco at
        Spoleto, Italy.

III. GENERAL REFERENCE WORKS

Die Alte Jungfer und der Dieb. Berlin: Interalliierte Musik-
leihbibliothek, 1943. 8 pp.
THE OLD MAID AND THE THIEF story and action,
scene by scene in German. At the end are review
excerpts from New Yorker, New York Post, New
York Mirror, Time, Newsweek, Philadelphia Bulletin and the Philadelphia Record. Orchestral
scoring is given.

American Society of Composers, Authors and Publishers Biographical Dictionary. 3rd ed. New York: ASCAP,
1966.
Who's Who sketch.

Americana Annual 1956. New York: Americana Corporation,
1956.
This short biographical article may have been included because Menotti won the 1954 Pulitzer Prize
in music for THE SAINT OF BLEECKER STREET.
Three paragraphs.

Apel, Willi and Ralph T. Daniel. The Harvard Brief Dic-
tionary of Music. Cambridge, Massachusetts: Harvard
University Press, 1960.
Short entries with plot summaries for AMAHL,
THE CONSUL, THE MEDIUM, and THE OLD MAID
(no summary for the latter).

Baker, Theodore. Biographical Dictionary of Musicians.
5th ed. New York: G. Schirmer, 1958.
Biographical sketch.

Bernard, Robert. Histoire de la Musique. Bourges, France:
Fernand Nathan, 1963. Vol. 3.
Biographical-critical article. Over a page in
length. Photos: Menotti coaching Amahl and Marie
Powers, Patricia Neway and Cornell MacNeil (?)

in the New York production of THE CONSUL in
1950.

Biancolli, Louis and Robert Bagar. The Victor Book of
    Operas. Revised ed. New York: Simon and Schuster,
    1953.
        Plot summaries of AMAHL, AMELIA, THE CON-
        SUL, and THE MEDIUM. The discography lists
        AMAHL. Photo: Eugene Berman's setting of
        AMAHL at the New York City Center.

Blum, David. A Pictorial Treasury of Opera in America.
    New York: Greenberg, 1954.
        Four photos: Rosemary Kuhlmann (Mother), Chet
        Allen (Amahl) and William Starling in AMAHL;
        Kuhlmann and the Three Kings in AMAHL; Marie
        Powers (Mother), Leon Lishner (Secret Police
        Agent) and Patricia Neway (Magda) in THE CONSUL;
        and Leo Coleman (Toby) and Marie Powers (Ma-
        dame Flora) in THE MEDIUM.

Bonaccorsi, Alfredo. Nuovo Dizionario Musicale. Milan:
    Curci, 1954.
        Brief biographical entry.

Briggs, John. Requiem for a Yellow Brick Brewery. New
    York: Little, Brown, 1969.
        Brief references and full page photo of Menotti.

Brockway, Wallace and Herbert Weinstock. The Opera: A
    History of Its Creation and Performance: 1600-1941.
    New York: Simon and Schuster, 1941.
        References to THE OLD MAID and the production
        of AMELIA at the Metropolitan Opera.

_____. The World of Opera: The Story of Its Origins and
    the Lore of Its Performance. New York: Pantheon
    Books, 1962.
        In "The Annals of Performance" the operas are
        AMELIA, THE CONSUL, and THE MEDIUM.
        Photo: THE MEDIUM in New York's Ethel Barry-
        more Theatre in 1947 with Marie Powers (Mme.
        Flora), Evelyn Keller (Monica) and Leo Coleman
        (Toby).

Bull, Storm. Index to Biographies of Contemporary Com-
    posers. New York: Scarecrow Press, 1964.

Eleven books are cited for Menotti.

_____. Index to Biographies of Contemporary Composers.
Volume II. Metuchen, N.J.: Scarecrow Press, 1974.
Twenty titles 1964-1973 given for Menotti.

Chase, Gilbert. America's Music from the Pilgrims to the
Present. New York: McGraw-Hill, 1955.
Summaries of THE MEDIUM, THE CONSUL and
AMAHL, plus critical commentary.

Collaer, Paul. La Musiques Moderne 1905-55. Brussels:
Elsevier, 1955.
Biographical information.

Collier's 1956 Year Book. New York: P. F. Collier & Son,
1956.
Biographical entry of two paragraphs.

Cooper, Martin, ed. The Concise Encyclopedia of Music and
Musicians. New York: Hawthorn Books, 1958.
Brief biographical note and brief entries for the
operas without specifics. Monochrome plate of
Menotti.

Cross, Milton. New Milton Cross' Complete Stories of the
Great Stories. Edited by Karl Kohrs. Revised and
enlarged edition. New York: Doubleday, 1955.
Detailed stories of AMAHL, THE MEDIUM and
THE SAINT with principal musical numbers indi-
cated.

Current Biography 1947. New York: H. W. Wilson, 1948.
Well written biographical article of over a page.
Excerpts from reviews of AMELIA, THE OLD
MAID, THE ISLAND GOD, THE TELEPHONE and
THE MEDIUM. Compact history of these operas.
With a list of sources. Photo of Menotti.

The Decca Book of Opera. London: Werner Laurie, 1956.
Biographical sketch and brief analysis by Felix
Aprahamian. Synopsis of THE CONSUL. THE
CONSUL is listed in the discography with full cast
listing.

Dictionary of American Contemporary Operas. New York:
Central Opera Service, 1967.

Very useful for any potential opera producer. The
information includes data on recordings, number of
acts and scenes, playing time for short works, cast
(voices), orchestration plus expected information
such as premiere dates. Thirteen works are listed.

Dizionario Ricordi della Musica e dei Musicisti.   Milan:
    Ricordi, 1959.
    Short entry with bibliography of works.

Dwyer, Terence. Opera in Your School.   London: Oxford
    University Press, 1964.
    AMAHL is included in a columnar table.   This
    opera "needs a good boy treble and good older
    girl. "

Eaton, Quaintance. The Miracle of the Met.   New York:
    Meredith Press, 1968.
    References to AMELIA, ISLAND GOD and LAST
    SAVAGE.

Eaton, Quaintance. Opera Production: A Handbook.   Minne-
    apolis: University of Minnesota Press, 1961.
    Information for AMAHL, AMELIA, THE CONSUL,
    THE SAINT, THE MEDIUM, THE TELEPHONE,
    THE OLD MAID and MARIA includes a synopsis,
    major roles with their range, lesser roles, chorus,
    bit parts, orchestra, production problems, avail-
    ability of rented materials, sources for photographs
    and performing companies of each work in the past.
    Very useful.

Encyclopedia della Musica.   Milan: Ricordi, 1963-64. vol. 3.
    Interpretative article, list of works and critical
    sources. Photo: G. Coltellaci's stage setting for
    AMAHL at the Florence Maggio Musicale in 1953.

Encyclopedia Salvat de la Musica.   Barcelona: Salvat Edi-
    tores, 1967: vol. 3.
    Article of over two columns with a list of works.
    Photos: AMELIA and Menotti.

Encyclopedia de la Musique.   Paris: Fasquelle, 1958-61.
    Article of over a page with bibliography of works.

Everyman's Dictionary of Music.   4th ed. London: J. M.
    Dent, 1962.

Brief biographical entry.

Ewen, David, ed. Composers Since 1900: A Biographical
and Critical Guide. New York: H. W. Wilson, 1969.
Five page biographical-critical article. The operas
receive careful analysis. Critical excerpts from
reviews are included. Brief bibliography. Photo
of Menotti.

_____. Encyclopedia of the Opera. New Edition. New
York: Hill and Wang, 1963.
Biographical sketch. Short summary of MARIA and
other operas.

_____. Ewen's Musical Masterworks: The Encyclopedia
of Musical Masterpieces. 2nd ed. New York: Bonanza
Books, 1954.
Background information and capsule summary of
AMAHL, AMELIA, THE CONSUL and THE MEDIUM.

_____. The New Book of Modern Composers. 3rd ed.
New York: Knopf, 1961.
Short biographical paragraph, a "Personal Note" by
Winthrop Sargeant, Menotti's article on opera and
theater from The New York Times Magazine, five-
page article on his operas and style by Robert
Sabin and references to his links with Wolf-Ferrari,
Puccini, Mascagni and Duparc. Comment on the
operas from AMELIA to MARIA.

Ewen, David. The New Encyclopedia of the Opera. New
York: Hill and Wang, 1971.
Biographical article and articles on the operas with
useful plot summaries. All are included except
THE MOST IMPORTANT MAN. Separate entries
for "I Shall Find You Shells, Stars, " the grand-
mother's lullaby, and "To This We've Come, "
Magda's aria from THE CONSUL.

Goldovsky, Boris. Bringing Opera to Life. New York:
Appleton-Century-Crofts, 1968.
Valuable stage direction for THE TELEPHONE.
Goldovsky instructs about "Ben's pantomime during
Lucy's first aria. " The author writes about drama,
the division of musical sections and coordinates the
pantomime with the dialogue. With seven musical
quotations and diagrams of the setting and stage
movements.

Graf, Herbert. Opera for the People. Minneapolis: Univer-
    sity of Minnesota Press, 1951.
        Section in "Opera on Broadway" plus many other
        references.   Photos: Horace Armistead's design
        for THE MEDIUM and Monica and Toby in the work
        at the Karama House Lyric Theatre in Cleveland
        directed by Benno D. Franklin.

Grout, Donald Jay. A Short History of Opera. New York:
    Columbia University Press, 1965. vol. 2.
        One excellent paragraph in "Tradition and Renewal."

Grove's Dictionary of Music and Musicians. Ed. by Eric
    Blom. 5th ed. New York: St. Martin's Press, 1954.
    vol. 5.
        Biographical article of over a page.

Hamm, Charles. Opera. Boston: Allyn and Bacon, 1966.
        References to the overture of THE TELEPHONE.
        Excerpt from Menotti's "A Note on the Lyric
        Theatre" concerning recitative.   Musical examples
        of recitative for Magda and the Secretary from THE
        CONSUL.   Illustration of Menotti's use of Metasta-
        sian, recitative-aria structure in the "To This
        We've Come" scene for Magda in THE CONSUL
        with the dialogue.   Photo of AMAHL on NBC-TV
        with Amahl, the Mother and the Magi.

Herzfeld, Friedrich.   Ullstein Musiklexikon.   Berlin: Ullstein,
    1965.
        Biographical entry and photo of Menotti.

Howard, John Tasker. Our American Music. 4th ed. New
    York: Thomas Y. Crowell, 1965.
        Biographical sketch of approximately three pages.
        Excerpts from reviews of THE ISLAND GOD,
        MARIA and LABYRINTH.

_____. The World's Great Operas. New York: Grosset
    and Dunlap, 1948.
        Plot summaries of AMELIA, THE ISLAND GOD,
        THE MEDIUM, THE OLD MAID and THE TELE-
        PHONE.

Jacobs, Arthur. A New Dictionary of Music. New York:
    Penguin Books, 1958.
        Very brief entry for Menotti, even shorter for the
        operas.

Kaufmann, Helen (Loeb). History's 100 Greatest Composers.
    New York: Grosset and Dunlap, 1957.
    One page biographical article with a drawing of
    Menotti. For teenagers.

Kerman, Joseph. Opera as Drama. New York: Knopf, 1956.
    Commentary on THE SAINT which is largely nega-
    tive as to the opera's dramatic worth.

Knapp, J. Merrill. The Magic of Opera. New York: Harper
    & Row, 1972.
    References to AMAHL. Paragraphs on Menotti's
    career. Brief excerpts from his "Note on the Lyric
    Theatre" on the recitative. Quotes from his
    article, "A Point of Contact." Photo of a HELP!
    production.

Kobbe's Complete Opera Book. Edited and revised by the
    Earl of Harewood. London: Putnam, 1958.
    Plot summaries and cast lists for THE MEDIUM,
    THE TELEPHONE and THE CONSUL.

Kolodin, Irving. The Metropolitan Opera 1883-1966: A Can-
    did History. New York: Knopf, 1966.
    Scattered references with brief commentary on
    AMELIA, THE CONSUL, THE ISLAND GOD, THE
    LAST SAVAGE, MARIA, THE MEDIUM, THE OLD
    MAID, THE SAINT and THE TELEPHONE. Ex-
    cerpts from New York newspaper reviews.

Lang, Paul Henry. Critic at the Opera. New York: Norton,
    1971.
    Excellent analysis of Menotti in "American Opera
    Native and Naturalized." Critic Lang says Menotti
    brings to America opera a new verismo, a new life.
    He relies on Italian musical ancestry (Puccini) and
    writes basically of passion. His biggest problem
    is that his music does not take command. His
    music is not effective as are his dramas and lib-
    rettos. Lang mentions without detail THE MEDIUM,
    AMELIA and THE CONSUL.

Larousse de la Musique. Paris: Larousse, 1957. vol. 2.
    Brief entry that mentions only THE MEDIUM and
    THE CONSUL.

Life International, eds. Nine Who Chose America. New

York: Dutton, 1959.
    An introductory article by Menotti and the article,
    "Renaissance Man of American Music" by Tom
    Prideaux which is excellent for its compact, simply
    stated view. Quotes by the composer on THE
    MEDIUM, some lines in Magda's aria from THE
    CONSUL. Each opera is discussed. For young
    adult readers. Photos: Menotti (full page), Menotti
    with Samuel Barber and another classmate before
    the Curtis Institute, the baby with his older brothers
    and sisters at Cadegliano, the villa overlooking
    Lake Lugano which was his childhood home, the
    ten-year-old Gian Carlo holding the bridal train of his
    sister Amalita, the composer seated on a slope of
    Monte Luco in Spoleto (full page) and dancers prac-
    ticing in the Spoleto square with children watching.

Lloyd, Norman. The Golden Encyclopedia of Music. New
    York: Golden Press, 1968.
        Biographical entry. Photos: Menotti with Samuel
        Barber, Aaron Copland, Virgil Thomson, William
        Schuman and by himself.

McSpadden, J. Walker. Operas and Musical Comedies. New
    York: Thomas Y. Crowell, 1946.
        Synopsis of AMELIA and THE ISLAND GOD.

Martin, George. The Opera Companion: A Guide for the
    Casual Operagoer. New York: Dodd, Mead, 1961.
        Very brief capsules of THE CONSUL, THE MEDIUM
        and THE TELEPHONE.

Mattfeld, Julius. A Handbook of American Operatic Pre-
    mieres, 1731-1962. Detroit: Information Service, Inc.,
    1963.
        Ten works are listed including THE UNICORN with
        playing length.

Matthews, Thomas. The Splendid Art: A History of the
    Opera. New York: Crowell-Collier Press, 1970.
        Several brief paragraphs of commentary. Menotti
        is quoted from Music and Musicians. Photo: Marie
        Powers (Mme. Flora), Evelyn Keller (Monica) and
        Leo Coleman (Toby) in THE MEDIUM.

Matz, Mary Jane. Opera: Grand and Not So Grand. New
    York: Morrow, 1966.

Valuable section in Chapter IX, "The Composer and
How He Works." Menotti is a unique opera composer in that he earns a livelihood on royalties
alone. He is mistrusted and criticized because he
appeals in an old-fashioned manner to a large audience. Critical excerpts from Stravinsky in Show,
Guido Pannain on THE CONSUL and AMAHL, Edmund Tracey on MARTIN'S LIE, Clarendon in Le
Figaro on THE LAST SAVAGE, Janet Flanner on
THE LAST SAVAGE in New Yorker and Jean Cocteau on THE MEDIUM. Matz, who is a former
associate of Menotti's, trails his hectic creative
routine during a seven month period in 1963-1964--
three premieres of THE LAST SAVAGE, the world
premiere of MARTIN'S LIE and plans for his Spoleto
festival. Menotti has remolded the operatic image.
Long runs, Broadway style, may be the answer for
contemporary opera.

Mayer, William. ICS Music Lecture on Contemporary
American Opera: A Survey of Its Development. Wash-
ington, D. C.: U. S. Information Agency, 1966.
In Part II, materials on Magda's climatic "To This
We've Come" and her suicide scene from THE
CONSUL. Mayer groups THE CONSUL with Jan
Meyerowitz's The Barrier as attacks on society.
AMAHL and LABYRINTH are mentioned as examples
of opera for television. LABYRINTH is the first
to use television photographic methods such as
flashbacks in a major way.

Merkling, Frank and editors of Opera News. The Golden
Horseshoe: The Life and Times of the Metropolitan
Opera House. New York: Viking Press (Studio Book),
1965.
Photo of Menotti at lunch with General Manager
Rudolph Bing and Robert Herman of the Met and the
Met production of THE LAST SAVAGE with George
London, Teresa Stratas, Ezio Flagello, Lili Chook-
asian, Roberta Peters, Nicolai Gedda and Morley
Meredith (Abdul's arrival in a cage).

Meyer's Handbuch uber die Musik. Mannheim: Bibliograph-
isches Institute, 1966.
Brief biographical entry.

Moore, Frank Leslie, comp. Crowell's Handbook of World

Opera. New York: Thomas Y. Crowell, 1961.
Brief plot summaries of AMAHL, AMELIA, THE
CONSUL, THE MEDIUM, THE OLD MAID and a
listing of the operas.

Moser, Jans Joachim.   Musik Lexikon.   Hamburg: Hans
Sikorski, 1951.
Brief biographical entry.

Die Musik in Geschichte und Gegenwart.   Basel: Barenreiter
Kassel, 1961. vol. 9.
Biographical article of over a column with a list of
works and sources.

Musikens Hvem Hvad Hvor.   Copenhagen: Politikens Forlag,
1950. vol. 2.
Who's Who article.   List of works.   Photo.

Musikens Hvem Hvad Hvor.   Copenhagen: Politikens Forlag,
1961. vol. 2.
Who's Who article.   List of works.

Opera Annual 1954-1955.   Ed. by Harold Rosenthal.   London:
John Calder, 1954.
Few sentences on Menotti's opera in Italy.   The
critics are largely negative in "Opera in Post-War
Italy" by Cynthia Jolly.

Opera Annual 1955-1956.   Ed. by Harold Rosenthal.   London:
John Calder, 1955.
Major consideration of THE SAINT by James Hinton,
Jr.   Despite its theatrical effectiveness the opera
does not make an entity.   Menotti has failed here
in plot and in characters.   Much of the action is
predictable.   Michele and Annina have no necessary
connection.   Michele is the center character but
does not have enough stature.   With the religious
ecstasy theme, Menotti fails to make his people
significant.   Photos: The first act of THE CONSUL
at Sadler's Wells with Olwen Price (Mother), Denis
Dowling (Police Agent) and Amy Shuard (Magda
Sorel); THE SAINT with Gloria Lane (Desideria)
accusing Davis Cunningham (Michele) as Gabriella
Ruggiero (Annina) holds his arm; and Davis Cunningham holding Virginia Copeland (Annina).

Opera Annual 1957-1958.   Ed. by Harold Rosenthal.   London:

John Calder, 1958.
Commentary in Charles Reid's "Now That Melody
Is Dead...." Reid admires THE CONSUL although
he notes Menotti is far from Puccini's musical
stature. Two paragraphs.

Opera Annual 1958-1959. Ed. by Harold Rosenthal. London:
John Calder, 1959.
Paragraph on MARIA and THE MEDIUM in "The
New York Season." Photo of MARIA at the World's
Fair in Brussels with Richard Cross (Donato),
Patricia Neway (Mother), Herbert Handt (Dr. Zuck-
ertanz) and Franca Duval (Maria).

Pauly, Reinhard. Music and the Theater. Englewood Cliffs,
New Jersey: Prentice-Hall, 1970.
Good analysis of THE CONSUL in "Two American
Operas." The theme of this opera can be identi-
fied with by a large audience. It is an indictment
against the effects of totalitarianism on people.
There are dramatic parallels between Tosca and
this work. Dream sequences are used to clarify
Magda's character. Contrast is used for emphasis.
An example is the French song at the beginning.
For the most part Menotti chooses effective language
to illustrate the coldness of bureaucracy. The
Secretary's character is even more important because of the Consul's absence. Magda's fate en-
gages our sympathies much more than her husband's. The music carries the drama almost
always. Recitatives are for the "dialogue of action"
and are as varied as the ensemble scenes are in
style. One is reminded of a radio orchestra in
Menotti's use of it as in the commentary after dia-
logues are finished. Even though the music is like
movie music, it contributes greatly to THE CON-
SUL's impact. Other brief references. Photos:
Full page of Magda and the Secretary in a San
Francisco production and a "All Documents Must
Be Signed" shot of Magda's aria with the Secretary
and two other women at the New York City Opera.

Peiper, Ethel and Marion Bauer. How Opera Grew From
Ancient Greece to the Present Day. New York: Put-
nam, 1956.
Comments in "American Innovators," mainly on
THE MEDIUM, THE CONSUL and THE SAINT. Ex-

cerpts from New York newspaper reviews.

Prawy, Marcel. The Vienna Opera. New York: Praeger,
    1970.
    One paragraph about the Adolf Rott production of
    THE CONSUL in 1951. Photo of THE CONSUL pro-
    duced in Vienna with Laszlo Szemere (Magician),
    Polly Batic (Vera Boronel) and Martha Rohs (Secre-
    tary).

Prieberg, Fred X. Lexikon der Neuen Musik.... Freiburg:
    Karl Alber, 1958.
    Four page article with excerpts from critical
    articles. Musical quotation from THE MEDIUM,
    "The sun has fallen and it lies in blood. " Photo
    of THE OLD MAID at Fernsehen in 1954.

Riemann, Hugo. Riemann Musik Lexikon. New York: Schott
    Music Corporation, 1961. vol. 3.
    Biographical entry of over half a column.

Rosenthal, Harold and John Warrack. Concise Oxford Dic-
    tionary of Opera. London: Oxford University Press,
    1964.
    Perceptive summation of the operas in an article of
    over a column. The entries for the operas are en-
    cyclopedic with no plot summary. An outstanding
    character such as Magda Sorel is given an entry.

Ruppel, Karl Hans. Music in Germany. Munich: F. Bruck-
    mann, 1952.
    Photos: THE MEDIUM and THE CONSUL at the Kiel
    City Theater.

Scholes, Percy A. Concise Oxford Dictionary of Music.
    London: Oxford University Press, 1952.
    Brief entries for the composer and AMELIA, THE
    CONSUL, THE ISLAND GOD, THE MEDIUM and
    THE TELEPHONE.

_____. Junior Oxford Companion to Music. London:
    Oxford University Press, 1954.
    Seven line entry and photo of Menotti.

_____. Oxford Companion to Music. 10th ed. London:
    Oxford University Press, 1970.
    Brief biographical entry.

Seltsam, William H. Metropolitan Opera Annals: A Chronicle
    of Artists and Performances. New York: H. W.
    Wilson, 1947.
        Cast listings for three performances of AMELIA in
        1937-38 season, three performances in 1938-39
        season and three performances of THE ISLAND
        GOD in the 1941-42 season. Pitts Sanborn's re-
        view of AMELIA, its premiere performance March
        3, 1938 in the New York World-Telegram. San-
        born feels AMELIA could have a good Metropolitan
        Opera history. He calls the score "delightful" but
        points out it is in the Italian tradition despite the
        English libretto. To Sanborn, Menotti in AMELIA
        is related to Wolf-Ferrari. The cast and conductor
        Ettore Panizza are praised; a filled house acclaims
        the new work.

Seltsam, William H. Metropolitan Opera Annals Second
    Supplement: 1957-1966. New York: H. W. Wilson,
    1968. listing
        Cast listings for seven performances of THE LAST
        SAVAGE in the 1963-64 season and for three in the
        1964-65 season. Harriet Johnson's New York Post
        review of THE LAST SAVAGE's Metropolitan pre-
        miere January 23, 1964. Four paragraphs.

Simon, Henry W. Festival of Opera. Garden City, New
    York: Hanover House, 1957.
        Plot summaries of AMAHL, AMELIA, THE CON-
        SUL, THE ISLAND GOD, THE MEDIUM, THE OLD
        MAID, THE SAINT and THE TELEPHONE. Other
        scattered references.

_____, ed. The Victor Book of the Opera. 13th ed.
    New York: Simon and Schuster, 1968.
        Admirable plot summations of AMAHL, THE MEDI-
        UM, and THE CONSUL. Photos: Amahl (Chet
        Allen) presents his crutch to the Magi as his mother
        watches; Chet Allen and Rosemary Kuhlmann
        (Mother) together; in THE CONSUL Patricia Neway
        (Magda) and Marie Powers (Mother) with the author-
        ities; the despairing Magda throwing forms in the
        air; in THE MEDIUM Marie Powers (Madame
        Flora) summons spirits for three clients; and Mme.
        Flora drives away her three clients and Toby (Leo
        Coleman) and Monica (Evelyn Keller).

Slonimsky, Nicholas. Music Since 1900. New York: Norton, 1937.
Notice of the first performance of AMELIA in Philadelphia.

Smith, Patrick J. The Tenth Muse: A Historical Study of the Opera Libretto. New York: Knopf, 1970.
Brief references to AMELIA, THE CONSUL and the librettos.

Thompson, Oscar, ed. International Cyclopedia of Music and Musicians. 9th ed. New York: Dodd, Mead, 1964.
Major interpretive article by critic Winthrop Sargeant. With bibliography of works.

_____. Plots of the Operas. New York: World, 1940.
Synopsis of AMELIA.

Thomson, Virgil. American Music Since 1910. New York: Holt, Rinehart & Winston, 1970.
Brief references to AMELIA, THE TELEPHONE and a skeletal sketch of Menotti with a bibliography of major works. Thomson's evaluation of Menotti is the final paragraph.

_____. Music Reviewed 1940-1954. New York: Vintage Books (division of Random House), 1967.
Composer's views on THE MEDIUM and THE TELEPHONE. He is always "enthralled" by THE MEDIUM and finds the other entertaining. One page.

_____. Music Right and Left. New York: Holt, 1951.
The composer's review from the New York Herald Tribune of THE CONSUL March 17, 1950. Thomson considers it as a "play of horror and deep pathos." He admires to a degree the way the score illustrates. For its music and drama he is most impressed by the final scene. He praises the cast, conductor and efficient production. Brief excerpt from an article by Tikhon Khrennikov in Sovietskove Iskusstov. Thomson speaks of the "pathological nature" of THE MEDIUM.

UNESCO. Films for Music Education and Opera Films: International Selective Catalogue. Comp. by International Music Centre, Vienna. Vienna: UNESCO, 1962.

THE MEDIUM is listed in "Opera Films." It is
85 minutes in length, 16 mm. and 35 mm. in
English.

Volbach, Walter R. Problems of Opera Production. 2d rev.
ed. New York: Archon Books, 1967.
Excerpts from a Menotti lecture on stage direction
at a National Theatre Conference.

Watson, Jack M. and Corinne. A Concise Dictionary of
Music. New York: Dodd, Mead, 1965.
Short biographical sketch.

Wechsberg, Joseph. The Opera. New York: Macmillan,
1972.
Short references to AMAHL, AMELIA, THE LAST
SAVAGE and Menotti's career.

Weisstein, Ulrich. The Essence of Opera. New York: Free
Press of Glencoe, 1964.
Brief commentary on THE CONSUL and a quote by
French composer Marcel Delannoy on the same.

Westermann, Gerhart von. Opera Guide. Ed. by Harold
Rosenthal. New York: Dutton, 1965.
Four page section, primarily the stories of THE
CONSUL and THE SAINT. Musical quotations from
the Magician's role in THE CONSUL.

Westrup, J. A. and F. A. Harrison. The New College Encyclopedia of Music. New York: Norton, 1960.
Brief biographical entry. His teachers are mentioned.

Who's Who in Music and Musician's International Directory.
5th ed. New York: Hafner, 1969.
Biographical sketch includes Menotti's awards,
teaching posts and address.

Young, Percy M. A Critical Dictionary of Composers and
Their Music. London: Dennis Dobson, 1964.
Short biographical sketch.

Zenei Lexikon. Budapest: Zenemu Kiado Vaillalat, 1965.
vol. 2.
Article of half a column. List of works.

IV. PERIODICAL ARTICLES
(by Opera)

AMAHL AND THE NIGHT VISITORS

"'Amahl and the Night Visitors.'" Etude, LXXII (December, 1954), 3 and the cover.
Three paragraphs of information in a box. Cover photo: Amahl (Bill McIver), the Mother (Rosemary Kuhlmann) and one of the Magi.

Bauch, J. N. "Menotti's Wondrous Legacy to Music Education." Music Educator's Journal, XLVII (September-October, 1960, n. 1), 112-114.
Stimulating article on the value of AMAHL to students of twelve, thirteen and fourteen. Bauch shows how the opera can become a class project.

Bellingardi, Luigi. "Rome." Opera, XXIII (June, 1972), 552.
Brief review of a double bill at the Teatro Dell' Opera in Rome. Bellingardi notes the validity of Menotti's music in contemporary theatre. AMAHL is a sizable success. Singers are mentioned for Amahl and the Mother. See also HELP!

Bloomfield, T. "Switzerland: Menotti Revival." Opera, XXIII (March, 1972), 269.
See also HELP!

Cincinnati Symphony Orchestra Program Notes, (December 21, 1956), 310-320.
Notes on AMAHL and other operas plus typical biographical notes. The notes begin with Menotti's explanation of how he came to compose the classic from his notes for the 1952 recording. He says AMAHL is for children. Menotti recalls how he and his little brother stayed awake in order to see the Three Kings. His favorite was King Melchior. When a commission came from NBC for a

40

television opera he had no ideas until he saw a
Hieronymus Bosch painting. In writing AMAHL he
did not think particularly of television but of an
"ideal stage. " To see his idea in the realism of
the theater is nightmarish for the creator. As
opposed to young people Menotti sees the stage as
closest to his "ideal theater, " catching more magic
than either cinema or television. The theater
should be a serious experience in which the spectator brings his best with him, quite unlike the
more casual television experience at home. Listening to recorded opera has the advantage of free
imagination with the disadvantages being primarily
physical ones. He recommends that his operas be
experienced in the theater.

"The Companion Presents a Family Theater. " Woman's
    Home Companion, LXXXIII (December, 1956), 107-112.
        Abridged text of the television script. Full page
    of costume cut-outs with directions on the opposite
    side and full page of parts of the stage setting with
    suggestions for lighting effects, lighting the stage,
    a tableau, making a curtain and preserving the cut-
    out theater. With a cut-out theater and characters.

Cowell, Henry. "Current Chronicle. " Musical Quarterly,
    XXXVIII (April, 1952), 296-298.
        Brief analysis of AMAHL with technical notes on the
    orchestration and a musical quotation from the
    Kings' song about the babe they seek. Brief com-
    ment on the NBC-TV production.

"Drug Store Opera. " International Musician, L (March,
    1952), 11-12.
        Brief review of an AMAHL performance February
    21 at Indiana University's East Hall.

Eaton, Quaintance. "Menotti's 'Amahl and the Night Visi-
    tors' Second Novelty of the Spring Season. " Musical
    America, LXXII (April 15, 1952), 5+.
        Sizable review of the first stage production of
    AMAHL in New York with THE OLD MAID April 9.
    On April 13 NBC-TV presents the original produc-
    tion again. Eaton contrasts the two, television and
    stage. Photo of the Eugene Berman production.
    See also THE OLD MAID.

_____. "New Menotti Opera Has Premiere on Christmas
Eve. " Musical America, LXXII (January 1, 1952),
3, 10.
In-depth review of the premiere television production. Eaton has revealing views on the plot, singing cast, dancers, the score, set and camera
work. Photos: Amahl (Chet Allen) playing his pipe
as his Mother is inside the house and the Magi and
Menotti rehearsing.

Favors, Aaron and Emmylou Krohn. "'Amahl and the Night
Visitors. '" Volta Review, LXIII (December, 1961),
484-485, 486+.
Article about an AMAHL production given at the
Iowa School for the Deaf. The problems are many.
How could it be presented to an audience of both
hearing and deaf children and adults? A speech
therapist simplifies the speaking roles. (The dialogue in the original version is given in columnar
form next to the modified version.) A printed
synopsis is provided for deaf members. Students
are chosen for Amahl and his mother who have
relatively intelligible speech. Individual instruction
is given through a compression amplifier for improving intelligibility. The RCA Victor album is
purchased and certain sections such as the overture
are taped for use in the performance. Photo of
the student Amahl and the student Mother in one
another's arms.

Geitel, Klaus. "Hamburg. " Neue Zeitschrift fur Musik,
CXXX (February, 1969), 54-55.
Review.

_____. "Hamburg: Wer hat Angst vor Globolinks?" Das
Orchester, XVII (March, 1969), 111-112.
Review of the first AMAHL at the Hamburg State
Opera. AMAHL has greater musical charm than
HELP! Menotti's coloring is delicately shaded.
The text and music are closely allied. The trio
for the Magi is well balanced. In the cast are
Jerry Jennings, William Workman, Noel Mangin,
Matthias Misselwitz (an effective Amahl) and Kerstin
Meyer (a dramatic Mother).
See also HELP!

Hamburger, Philip. "Television. " New Yorker, XXVII

(January 5, 1952), 56+.
Review of the first television production. Hamburger praises the opera. He tells of Menotti's inspiration to compose AMAHL. Plot summary. Over two columns.

Hijman, Julius. "Een Televisie-Opera van Menotti. " Mens En Melodie, VIII (January, 1953), 4-7.
Review. Photos: Amahl presents his crutch to the Magi in the NBC-TV production and the Mother attempting to steal the gold in the Netherlands' production.

Holde, A. "'Amahl und die Nachtlichen Gaste. '" Musikleben, V (December, 1952), 374-375.
Review of the NBC-TV production. The style is that of the mystery play. The music is never trivial. Its religious tone is rare in modern works. Holde gives Menotti's inspiration for the opera. Necessarily different lighting has been used for television. Acoustical problems of recording moving singers have been mostly solved by using more recording machinery. Plot summary.

"Holiday Music. " International Musician, L (December, 1951), 36.
Menotti's comments on the AMAHL libretto before the television premiere.

"Indiana University Stages New Operas. " Musical Courier, CXLV (March 15, 1952), 23.
Review of the first stage presentation of AMAHL February 21 at Indiana University. Local critics praise it and the young cast. An Indiana boy sings Amahl after winning a state-wide series of auditions.

Joachim, Heinz. "Hamburg. " Opera, XX (March, 1969), 236-237.
Review. Menotti stages the opera. See also HELP! HELP!

Kirstein, Lincoln. "Television Opera in U. S. A. " Opera, III (April 1952), 201-202.
Review. The opera is a triumph on NBC television. Three paragraphs on the television production. Photo of the production.

Kolodin, Irving. "'Amahl' and 'Elizah' Join 'Parsifal' in the
    Easter Parade. " Saturday Review, XXX (April 26,
    1952), 30.
        Review of AMAHL at the City Center. Two para-
        graphs.

_____. "Menotti's 'Amahl' on TV. " Saturday Review,
    XXX (January 12, 1952), 30.
        Review of Menotti's "most accomplished score" on
        NBC-TV Christmas Eve, 1951.

Levinger, Henry W. "First Opera Written for Television
    Bows. " Musical Courier, CXLV (January 1, 1952), 5.
        Review of the AMAHL world premiere. To
        Levinger it is a masterpiece. On the telecast the
        composer explains his inspiration. Photo of Chet
        Allen as Amahl playing a shepherd's pipe in re-
        hearsal.

_____. "NBC-TV Presents 'Amahl. '" Musical Courier,
    CLI (January 1, 1955), 40.
        Short review of the NBC-Opera Theatre television
        production one week before the opening of THE
        SAINT on Broadway.

McDonald, Dennis. "'Amahl' Hit; Repeats TV Success at
    NYC Opera. " Billboard, LXIV (April 19, 1952), 48.
        Enthusiastic review of the production at the New
        York City Opera. It ought to become a classic.
        Real emotions lift the work. McDonald praises the
        designer, conductor and choreographer. Brief plot
        summary. See also THE OLD MAID.

Marks, Marcia. Dance Magazine, XLIV (March, 1970), 86.
        Review of one paragraph of a City Center per-
        formance.

Marx, Henry. "Failure and Success at the City Center. "
    Music News, XLV (May 1952), 4.
        Review of the City Center production. Marx says
        Menotti continues to grow in integrating music and
        action while pushing drama to the fore. The music
        is among his finest. Amahl as a character is a
        continuation of THE MEDIUM's Monica. Berman's
        setting is beautiful yet practical. See also THE
        OLD MAID.

"Menotti and Television. " Newsweek, XXXIX (January 7,
1952), 36-37.
Review of the world premiere performance. Newsweek feels the excellent production augurs well for
the future of television opera. Photo from the production of Amahl, the Mother and the Three Kings.

"Menotti Opera is Now a Christmas Classic. " Life, XXXIII
(December 15, 1952), 102-103.
Five color photos of the City Center production with
Eugene Berman sets. The cast is Rosemary Kuhl-
mann (Mother, M. Pollock, Richard Wentworth and
Lawrence Winters (The Three Kings) and Mary
Hinkson (dancing role of Shepherdess).

"Menotti Opera Makes Television History. " Musical America,
LXXIV (January 1, 1954), 27.
Short article about the fourth annual television performance December 20. This is the first commercial color telecast in history.

"Menotti Tries Again. " Time, LXI (May 25, 1953), 50.
Review. AMAHL in Florence's Pergola Theater.
The public gives ten curtain calls to a performance.
Newspaper reviews are mixed. In Rome Il Tempo
is unfavorable while Milan's Corriere della Sera is
favorable.

"Menotti's 'Amahl' Staged at New York City Center. " Musical
Courier, CXLV (May 1, 1952), 11.
Review of the first Manhattan stage performance.
See also THE OLD MAID.

Miller, Philip L. "Especially for Christmas a New 'Amahl.'"
American Record Guide, XXXI (December, 1964), 296.
Review of the RCA Victor recording. Stereo's
advent called for a new AMAHL. After misgivings
Menotti is delighted with the new recording. The
cast: Kurt Yaghjian (Amahl), Martha King (Mother),
John McCollum (Kaspar), Willis Patterson (Balt-
hazar), Richard Cross (Melchior), Julian Patrick
(Page) and the conductor, Herbert Grossman. Photo
of the Magi and their Page and Amahl and his
Mother.

Miller, Philip L. "The Original Cast 'Amahl. '" American
Record Guide, XXXVII (December, 1970), 208-209.

Review of the first recording by RCA Victor.
Miller is impressed by Chet Allen (Amahl) and
Rosemary Kuhlmann (Mother) and notes that it can
probably never be superseded. Others in the recording are Andrew McKinley (Kaspar), David Aiken (Melchior) and Frank Monachino (Page).
Thomas Schippers conducts on RCA Victrola 1512.

"Miracle at the Crossroads. " International Musician, L
(January, 1952), 12-13.
Review which is almost adulatory about the pre-
miere television production. Verses for the Magi,
Amahl and the Mother are quoted.

"Ninth Radio Poll Reflects Growing Status of Television. "
Musical America, LXXII (June 1, 1952), 3.
AMAHL places first as the "Outstanding Work of
Any Type" in the magazine's annual poll of music
on the air. It is runner-up for "Outstanding Event
of the Year. "

"On Television. " Opera, XIX (February, 1968), 172.
Review of the opera on BBC television December
26, 1967. Two paragraphs.

Romagnoli, Mary. "Looking Ahead in 1953. " Choral Guide,
VI (February, 1953), 28-30.
Review of AMAHL at the First Methodist Church in
Yonkers, New York. Romagnoli considers the
opera a classic and believes this performance is
the first to use a church.

"Sentimental Journey. " House and Garden, CII (December,
1952), 116-117.
Article of one page. With Eugene Berman's hand-
some original water-color sketches.

Shanet, Howard. "Out of the Mouths of Babes. " Music
Clubs Magazine, XXXII (January, 1953), 4-5, 22.
Delightful article by the conductor of the Hunting-
don, West Virginia symphony orchestra describing
a community production. Useful for anyone planning
a community production.

Storrer, William. "Hempstead, Long Island. " Opera, XV
(February, 1964), 98-99.
Review of a modern dress production given by

Hofstra University.   One paragraph.

Sutcliffe, James H.   "Menotti's Globolinks. "   High Fidelity/
    Musical America, (April, 1969), MA 27-28.
        Brief notice of a Hamburg production.   See also
        HELP!

"There Were Three Kings. "   Colliers, CXXX (December 27,
    1952), 92-93.
        Article about the second televising of AMAHL.   The
        cast is the same as the first year's except for a
        new Amahl (Bill McIver).   Nine color photos of the
        NBC-TV production.

"Three Kings in 50 Minutes. "   Time, LVIII (December 31,
    1951), 30.
        Review of the world premiere televising.   Plot
        summary and inclusion of four lines for Melchior
        beginning, "Oh, woman you can keep the gold. "
        Five paragraphs.   Photo of Menotti directing Rose-
        mary Kuhlmann and Chet Allen.

Torday, S.   "Maggio Musicale te Florence. "   Mens en
    Melodie, VIII (June, 1953), 223-224.
        Review of AMAHL at the Florence May festival.
        Two paragraphs.   Photo of Leopold Stokowski
        (Conductor) with the cast (Guilietta Simionato is the
        Mother).

Wagner, K.   "Kaviar fuers Kindervolk.... "   Melos, XXXVI
    (February, 1969), 79-81.
        Review of the Hamburg production.   See also
        HELP!

Watts, Douglas.   "Large and Small. "   New Yorker, XXVIII
    (April 19, 1952), 91.
        Review of the City Center production.   He praises
        the Eugene Berman set and costumes.   He is en-
        thusiastic about AMAHL.   See also THE OLD
        MAID.

"Weinachtliche Legende. "   Musica (Basel), VI (January, 1953),
    26-27.
        Review of a Wiesbaden performance.   Compared to
        earlier Menotti the melody is simple.   Four short
        paragraphs.   Plot summary.   Photo of the produc-
        tion with Amahl, the Mother and the Magi.

Wyatt, Euphemia van Renssalaer. Catholic World, CLXXV
(June, 1952), 227-228.
Review of AMAHL at the City Center. Wyatt says
Menotti adds warmth by giving personal dimensions
to the Magi.

AMELIA GOES TO THE BALL [Amelia al Ballo]

Bellingardi, L. "Rome. " Opera, XVIII (July, 1967), 584.
Short review of a successful AMELIA at the Rome
Opera.

Brindle, Reginald. "New Operas in Triple Bill at La Scala."
Musical America, LXX (April, 1954), 7.
Brief mention of a successful AMELIA.

"Gian-Carlo Menotti's L'Opera-bouffe 'Amelia al Ballo. "
Disques, LXXVII (January-February, 1956), 78.
Article and review of the Columbia recording. The
writer is favorable toward AMELIA if not toward
THE CONSUL or AMAHL. He is critical of the
"socialist tendencies" of certain later works.
AMELIA and THE TELEPHONE are closest to the
"real" Menotti. Menotti has good comic observa-
tions in AMELIA. Mentioned are the husband's
scene with the lover, Amelia's prayer and the
"Pirandellian" trio. The music is called "exquisite."
The recording is praised as are members of La
Scala. Brief plot summary. Nino Sanzogno conducts. Four large paragraphs.

Hinton, James Jr. "Menotti: 'Amelia al Ballo. '" High
Fidelity, IV (February, 1955), 63.
Review of the recording. AMELIA has become a
historic opera. This opera buffa has many musical
debts, but its libretto is very much of this century
in amorality. It is never dull. The recording has
style. Three paragraphs. Photo of Menotti.

Jolly, Cynthia. "Menotti's 'Amelia' Heard in Rome. "
Musical America, LXXVII (March, 1957), 47.
Review. Two paragraphs.

Liebling, Leonard. "Curtis Institute of Music Sponsors Opera
Premieres. " Musical Courier, CXV (April 10, 1937),
7+.

Review. AMELIA is a great success, warmly
praised by Liebling. He also praises the libretto.
He considers the music charming. Good plot summary. Photos: Margaret Daum (Amelia) and
Leonard Treash (Police Officer) in the finale and
an earlier scene involving the chorus.

"Light Opera at Munich. " Opera, XVI (March, 1965), 202-
203.
Cast listing of a production at the Cuvilies Theater.
Photo: the Munich production with Ingeborg Hall-
stein (Amelia), Keith Engen (Husband) and David
Thar (Lover).

Mari, Pierrette. "Creation 'D' 'Amelia va au Bal' au Cours
d'un Gala Menotti a Metz. " Journal Musical Francais, CLXVIII (April, 1968), 40-41.
Review of AMELIA at Metz, France. AMELIA recalls the past masters of bel canto. Mari finds
influences of Manon, Carmen and Tosca's prayer
in this comic opera. The music and an orchestration sometimes too heavy add up to an agreeable
musical comedy. At a rehearsal the Amelia struck
her husband's head so hard with a vase that baritone Jacques Herbillon was really taken to a hos-
pital. The stage director Raymond Armond is
imaginative in finding the appropriate tone and rhy-
thm. Jacques Herbillon as an excellent husband
dominates the cast. Other cast members are listed.
Musically THE MEDIUM is stronger. Plot summary. Eight paragraphs. Photos: Karen Mesavage
(Amelia) with Janine Capderou (Maid) and Mesavage
and Michel Caron (Lover).

"Modern One-Act Works Score Success in Philadelphia. "
Newsweek, XLII (April 10, 1937), 19.
Short review of AMELIA at the Philadelphia Academy of Music. Menotti is striving for a new simplicity; the overture sparkles. The audience is
enthusiastic. Plot summary. Photo of Menotti.

"Opera Can Be Fun. " Time, LI (April 19, 1948), 50.
Review. AMELIA on a double bill. Audience reaction is good. See also THE OLD MAID.

Sargeant, Winthrop. "Musical Events. " New Yorker, XXXIX
(May 18, 1963), 96.

Review of a double bill at the New York City Opera.
Sargeant is very entertained by AMELIA and sees
in it Menotti's early talent, in fact, an early mastery
of his profession.   See also THE MEDIUM.

Schmidt-Garre, H.   Neue Zeitschrift fur Musik, CXXVI (Feb-
     ruary, 1965), 69-70.
          Brief review.   Photo of Ingeborg Hallstein (Amelia)
          and Karl Christian Kohn (Police Commissioner).

_____. "Mit 'Rita' und 'Amelia' ins Neue Jahr." Das
     Orchester, XIII (March, 1965), 87-88.
          Review of a Munich production.   This is Menotti's
          most elegant work.   The chorus is best in the
          finale.   Photo of Ingeborg Hallstein (Amelia) and
          Karl Christian Kohn (Police Commissioner).

Smith, Cecil.   "Music: Operatic Gagster." New Republic,
     CXVIII (April 26, 1948), 36-37.
          Review at the New York City Center.   Smith notes
          that Menotti treats feminine foibles often.   AMELIA
          seems to Smith to be a more careful work than
          THE OLD MAID.   Comment on the permanence of
          the operas.   See also THE OLD MAID.

THE CONSUL

Aprahamian, Felix.   World Review, XLVIII (?), (April, 1951),
     58-61.
          Perceptive review of the Cambridge Theatre pro-
          duction in London.   London has kept up with this
          new work after its slight notice of THE TELE-
          PHONE and THE MEDIUM.   This is a more serious
          work than the earlier operas and is "irresistable."
          Menotti's use of contrast is expert.   Several para-
          graphs illustrate these contrasts--light relief setting
          off tension.   A lullaby sung by the grandmother is
          followed by Magda's nightmare.   Waltz music for
          the hypnotized waiters is followed by Magda's ago-
          nizing "My name is woman" scene.   Act Three is a
          rich illustration of musical and dramatic contrasts.
          Despite Menotti's concern with prosody, his talent
          for ensembles is obvious.   The final ten bars are
          the flaw, dramatically out of place.   The critic is
          reminded of Alban Berg's revision of Wozzeck's
          final three bars.   Talking to the London Opera

Circle, Menotti discusses the "originals" of the in-
coherent foreign woman, the Magician and the old
Italian woman. The cast makes a tremendous
impact.

Ardoin, John. Musical America, LXXXII, (May, 1962), 25.
THE CONSUL is still important at the New York
City Opera. A new stage director, Roger Englander, adds some new touches. Patricia Neway
repeats her brilliant role.

Baldini, G. "'Il Console' di G. C. Menotti." Rassegna
Musicale, XXXII, (n. 2-4, 1962), 242-247.
Includes a bibliography.

Barraud, Henry. "Contrasting Modern Operas Hold Parisian
Stages." Musical America, LXXI (October, 1951), 6.
Review of THE CONSUL as performed in Paris in
English.

Bayliss, Stanley. "'The Consul.'" Musical Times, XCVIII
(December, 1957), 679.
Review of two paragraphs of a revival at Sadler's
Wells. He finds it much too melodramatic and un-
moving.

Benjamin, Arthur. Music and Letters, XXXII (July, 1951),
247-251.
Careful analysis. Benjamin begins with a plot summary. He thinks it is a rare blending of "drama,
music, and performance." He has high praise for
the text and Menotti's inventions such as the popular
French song played in Act I. The opera is "melodrama" in the proper sense of combining opera and
drama. While Menotti is not original, he has
facility in eclectic music, some of which is powerful. He lists ten main set pieces which illustrate
that the music is not "cinema." Neway is outstanding as Magda. Benjamin finds the music for the
final vision too sentimental. THE CONSUL is a
towering achievement. Synopsis.

Brahms, Caryl. "By the Waters of Babylon." Halle (Man-
chester), XLVI (April, 1951), 6-10.
Strongly stated review at the Cambridge Theater in
London. He says it is a theatrical work, not a
"work of art." He finds the Italian ancestry to his

liking. It is not as tart as THE MEDIUM since it
lacks coherency due to Menotti's angered state.
Magda's suicide is anti-climactic since it is so an-
ticipated. Menotti sometimes has to force syllables
to fit the music. The cast is the new breed of the
singer-actor. With quotes from the libretto.
Photos: Marie Powers (Mother), Patricia Neway
(Magda) and Leon Lishner (Chief Agent) in the first
act and Gloria Lane (Secretary) and Norman Kelley
(Magician).

Brindle, R. S. "Italy." Musical Times, XCV (March, 1954),
150-151.
Review of a production at the San Carlo in Naples.
Brindle finds the opera intense as drama. One
paragraph.

Brown, John Mason, "Man's Inhumanity." Saturday Review,
XXXII (April 22, 1950), 28-30.
Review by a drama critic. Brown voted for THE
CONSUL as the Best Musical (New York Drama
Critics Circle). He says the text could stand by
itself. THE MEDIUM was sheer melodrama. THE
CONSUL has a greater purpose and theme. To
Brown, this is the tragedy of people trapped by
"red tape." There are many villains, some of
them unintentional. Most of us, like the Secretary,
are numbed by mass catastrophe. Because the
people she faces daily have become impersonal, the
Secretary's reactions have become indifferent.
Menotti contrasts group suffering with individuals
such as Magda. Photo of Magda and John Sorel
(Patricia Neway and Cornell MacNeil).

Clurman, Harold. "Bali Hai." New Republic, CXXII (April
10, 1950), 21-22.
Review. The reviewer notes how the audience is
socially moved, that Menotti appeals because he
combines earlier Italian operatic melodrama with
topical themes. Clurman feels the work does not
measure up to earlier models while noting that the
audience's reaction is a good defense for THE
CONSUL. The cast is praised.

" 'The Consul.' " Life, XXVIII (April 10, 1950), 61-63.
Three paragraph article. Photos: Magda (Patricia
Neway) and the Mother (Marie Powers) refusing to

tell the secret police where Sorel is; the Magician
hypnotizing the waiting people into dancing; the
Mother singing a lullaby to the dying child; Magda
tearing up the consulate papers; and Magda joining
her husband, mother and the people in a dream-
death dance.

'"The Consul. '" Musical Times, XCII (April, 1951), 166.
Review of a production which opened February 7 at
the Cambridge Theater in London. The operatic
technique is called Italian verismo. The opera is
believed theatrically effective. Plot summary and
cast listing.

'"The Consul. '" Theatre Arts, XXXIV (March, 1950), 28-29.
Article which discusses the efforts of Chandler
Cowles and Efrem Zimbalist, Jr. to raise money
for the Broadway production by having auditions for
possible investors. The inspiration for the work is
explained. Photos: the score and working notes;
Menotti outlining the plot; Neway; the audition audience; Cowles and Zimbalist with designer Horace
Armistead and lighting expert Jean Rosenthal;
Menotti showing Cowles and Armistead the scale
model of the set and Menotti listening to auditions.

_____, XXXIV (May, 1950), 17.
Review with plot summary. The theme is about
the loss of freedom in bureaucracy. Two outstand-
ing scenes balance certain banalities. Patricia
Neway is called a new star for her Magda. Com-
plete credits for the cast and production team.
Photos: the Mother (Marie Powers) and Magda; the
Foreign Woman (Maria Marlo) and Mr. Kofner
(George Jongeyans).

'"The Consul' at the Cambridge Theater. " The Strad, LXI
(April, 1951), 412.
Review of the London production. It impresses the
critic more than any opera since Peter Grimes.
One sizable paragraph.

'"Consul' Preem in Vienna Top Event of Year. " Variety,
CLXXXII (March 14, 1951), 15.
Review of a Vienna State Opera production. The
Viennese speculate over which country Menotti in-
tends in his attack on bureaucracy. It is charged

that Communists were involved in the opera's con-
troversy at La Scala.

"Current Chronicle. " Musical Quarterly, XXXVI (December
15, 1950), 447-450.
Analysis. Musical examples of recitative, a tune
in the lullaby and the orchestral background. Effective and brief consideration of the opera.

Danzus, Domenico. "'Il Console' di Menotti al Teatro Mas-
simo di Catania. " Musica d'Oggi, IV (July-August,
1961), 180-182.
Review. The cast includes Clara Petrella, Piero
Guelfi, Jolanda Gardino. Ten paragraphs.

Darack, Arthur. "'The Consul. '" Cincinnati Symphony Program Notes (November 8, 1957), 181-208.
Thoughtful analysis of THE CONSUL and other biographical material. A newspaper account of a
woman's suicide over failure to get a visa is the
springboard for the opera. It protests indifference
to human oppression. There is great force in the
composer's examination of one incident. This is a
melodrama that is dreadful in its atmosphere of inhumanity and doom. The psychology back of the
melodrama is familiar. Yet it is this familiarity
that forces Menotti to go beyond the "mechanics of
suffering. " Darack discusses briefly Menotti's
ability in stage direction and linguistics. There
are three paragraphs from program notes for the
RCA recording (LM 1701) of AMAHL explaining
Menotti's views of the theater. In this passage
Menotti says he first conceives of all his operas
on an ideal stage disassociated from reality. Unlike Verdi, Menotti can go outside of convention in
the American musical stage with numerous choices
to make. His music is heavily eclectic. Excerpts
from Henry Cowell's review in Musical Quarterly
about the general style. The notes end with a plot
summary divided by scenes and acts including notes
on the orchestra music, set pieces (quintet, aria,
etc.) and quoted dialogue.

"De Nederlandse Opera. " Mens en Melodie, XI (April, 1956),
117-119.
Review. Photo of Louise de Vries (Secretary), Jan
van Mantgem (Secret Agent) and Gerard Holthaus

(John Sorel).

Frankenstein, Alfred. "Hebrew 'Consul.'" Opera, XXII
(July, 1971), 632.
Review of a Jaffa, Israel production April 12 sung
in Hebrew. Menotti is successful in motivating the
singers to act. Two paragraphs.

Garde, Carlos O. "Reposiciones en el Colon, 'El Consul, '
vibrantes valores teatrates." Buenos Aires Musicale,
XXII (May 2, 1967), 3.

"Gian-Carlo Menotti." Pan Pipes. XLIV (January, 1952), 39.
Article of four paragraphs. Photo of the opera at
the University of Minnesota in October, 1951.

"Gian-Carlo Menotti's Muziektheater." Mens en Melodie, VII
(February, 1952), 54-55.
Thorough plot summary divided by acts in relation
to a Dutch production. Profile photo of Menotti.
See also GENERAL.

Goury, Jean. "A Annecy: un 'Consul' 'Kafkaien.'" Opera
(France), X (n. 87, 1970), 14-15.
Review article of THE CONSUL. The production
is by Antoine Golea. Rene Terrasson accents the
"Kafkaian dimension" in the consulate scenes.
Goury thinks the director has solved the opposite
of realism and symbolism well. Michele Herbe
brings strong identification to Magda Sorel. Claude
Meloni's John Sorel is also praised. Other cast
members are not at their high level, but most are
adequate to their roles. Other cast members are
Georges L. Miazza (Magician), G. Privez (Police-
man), Christa Andersen (Italian Woman), Josette
Jacques (Mother) and Paulette Simard (Secretary).
The orchestra from the municipal theatre of Gre-
noble is hindered by the small setting. Rene
Begou conducts. Photo of Claude Meloni (Sorel),
Michele Herbe (Magda) and Josette Jacques (Mother).

Haggin, B. H. Nation, CLXX (June 3, 1950), 557-558.
Review. Haggin says the form is not new, that
Menotti's "pre-modern" style of melody is inade-
quate for such climactic times as "To this we've
come." He attributes its success to the drama
despite some pleasing music. The opera is musical

drama and could be successful in the opera house
as well. He denies the opera is "first-class" as
Winthrop Sargeant calls it.

Hell, Henri. La Revue Musicale, CCXI (March, 1952), 7-9.
Criticism. The opera centers on an epoch. Menotti
could make his point with added reserve, but the
audience responds as he wishes. Action is primary over the music which complements, makes
atmosphere and comments. The music's position-
ing is good. Hell questions if the music should
rule in order to retain its former stance with the
action secondary to it and if THE CONSUL's style
will become a fixture of contemporary music drama.

Jacobs, Arthur. "California Postscript." Opera, XX,
(August, 1969), 692-693.
Review at the San Francisco Spring Opera. Jacobs
thinks the music is more supportive than dominant.
He praises the cast. Photo of Jeannine Crader
(Magda) and Joshua Hecht (Secret Agent).

_____. Opera, XX, (September, 1969), 815-816.
Review with the London Opera Centre at Sadler's
Wells Theatre. The production is criticized for its
dullness. The critic illustrates two examples of
student singers singing phrases incorrectly ruining
the dramatic sense. For the most part the singing
fails to make its desired impact.

Joachim, Heinz. "Menotti's 'Konsul.'" Melos, XVIII, (Feb-
ruary, 1951), 52-53.
Review of a production at the Hamburg Staatsoper.
Joachim doubts if it will be a lasting success in
Germany. The main problem is the music. Four
paragraphs.

Jurik, M. "Cs. Premiera Menottiho." Hudebni Rozhledy,
XIX (n. 15, 1968), 465.

Kaczynski, Tadeusz. "Warszawski 'Konsul.'" Ruch Muzyczny, XVI (n. 5, 1972), 6-7.
Review. Photos: Krystyna Szczepanska (Mother)
and Krystyna Jamroz (Magda) in the first act of the
Warsaw production and an Act II setting.

Kanski, J. Ruch Myzyczny, VI (n. 7, 1962), 17.

Illustrated.

Kastendieck, Miles. "'The Consul.'" Christian Science
    Monitor Magazine, (March 25, 1950), 5.
        Review. THE CONSUL stirs its audiences. With
        this work Menotti becomes the hope of future opera.
        Bureaucracy's indifferent procedure is a central
        theme. Some of the devices are ordinary but are
        handled with real feeling. The excellent cast helps
        to depict the work's nobility. Photo of Patricia
        Neway and Cornell MacNeil.

Kirstein, Lincoln. "Menotti's 'The Consul.'" Opera, II,
    (March, 1951), 175-178.
        Analysis. It is the most successful musical work
        since Porgy and Bess. Kirstein suggests Virgil
        Thomson should not have called it less than first
        rate. He believes that despite its popularity THE
        CONSUL is a work of real worth. M. Francis
        Poulenc says the defect is that the music is not the
        dominant element. His colleagues sometimes re-
        sent his success. THE CONSUL may illustrate that
        counter-revolutionary works are the new order.
        Menotti's simple means along with his real anger
        make it an extraordinarily appealing work. While
        the ending may not be the best curtain, it has a
        "certain inevitable conviction." One is forced to
        admire theatre of great warmth and lack of preten-
        siousness. Photo of Neway (Magda) and Powers
        (Mother) in the New York production.

Kolodin, Irving. "'The Consul' for Ear Alone." Saturday
    Review, XXXIII (October 28, 1950), 74.
        Review of the Decca opera recording. Kolodin says
        Decca captures the theatricality of the opera. He
        notes that the music for the Act II vision is thin
        and that the score has both very good music and
        some "trite" melodramatic stretches. Menotti's
        own talents sometimes lead him to musical cheap-
        nesses. Kolodin praises the excellent reproduction
        of the composer's conception.

_____. "Menotti Moves Ahead." Saturday Review, XXXII
    (March 25, 1950), 62-63.
        Thoughtful analysis. Kolodin says Menotti has
        grown greatly as a composer. Good consideration
        of THE CONSUL's story and casting.

Krutch, Joseph Wood. Nation, CLXX (April 1, 1950), 305.
    Commentary on the work as drama. Krutch thinks
    the term "musical drama" is accurate. The great-
    est communication comes from the music, not the
    libretto. Plot summary.

"Letter to the Editor. " Music and Letters, XXXII (October,
    1951), 400.
    The writer says Arthur Benjamin reacts as a lay-
    man to THE CONSUL, that he (the writer) feels his
    feelings are played upon by pathetic happenings on
    the stage. He does not think the opera is a "work
    of art. " Three paragraphs.

Levinger, Henry W. "Menotti's 'The Consul' Bows on Broad-
    way. " Musical Courier, CXLI (April 1, 1950), 7.
    Extremely favorable review at the Ethel Barrymore
    Theatre. Levinger summarizes each act's story
    and discusses Menotti as composer, librettist and
    stage director. Photos: the Mother, the Magician
    hypnotizing Magda and Magda in the final scene.

"Light and Heavy. " Opera News, XXIV (March 12, 1960),
    27-28.
    Review of THE CONSUL at the New York City
    Opera. The reviewer who heard the opera ten
    years earlier is less moved this time.

Lockspeiser, Edward. "Menotti's 'The Consul' Has Pre-
    mieres in Two European Musical Centers. " Musical
    America, LXXI (April 1, 1951), 9.
    Review of productions in London and Vienna. In
    London the writer reports some critics overlook
    the opera's music in their study of its drama.
    Menotti has abosrbed many influences in an original
    manner. Lockspeiser feels his "most striking
    gift" to be finding the equivalent of speech for the
    voice.

Marx, Henry. "Menotti's 'Consul' Triumphs on Broadway. "
    Music News, XLII (June, 1950), 25.
    Full page review. It is one of the most powerful
    dramas since Tiefland over forty years ago. To
    lighten the grimness he introduces a magician.
    His music remains highly eclectic with suggestions
    of Puccini and d'Albert. His best music comes in
    the instrumental passages. THE CONSUL's ele-

ments are superior to THE MEDIUM's. Menotti's
staging adds greatly to the work. Patricia Neway
as Magda achieves a great feat despite certain
vocal harshnesses. The rest of the cast is generally successful.

"Menotti Flayed. " Time, LVII (February 5, 1951), 38.
Article about the work at La Scala. There is an
extremely varied reaction from the public, bravos
against boos. With small quotes from reviews in
the Communist Unita and Corriere della Sera in
Milan.

Montagu, George. "Gian-Carlo Menotti's 'The Consul' at the
Cambridge Theater. " London Musical Events, VI
(March, 1951), 20-22.
Review. Menotti uses several musical styles. A
magician provides some relief from its grimness.
The cast is excellent as is the conductor. Capsule
plot summary. Photos: Gloria Lane, David Aiken,
Maria Marlo and Patricia Neway in the consulate;
John Sorel (Russell George) bidding farewell to
Magda (Neway) with the Mother (Marie Powers) and
the Act I finale.

"Opera Diary. " Opera, II (April, 1951), 262-265.
Review. The critic feels that Menotti lacks the
means to express his feelings. He thinks it is more
a dramatic than musical success. Menotti has
strong theatrical instincts in THE CONSUL. The
American cast is praised for its interpretations.
Photos of the London production: Neway and Powers
on the cover; Russell George (John Sorel) and
Neway; Leon Lishner (Secret Police Agent) and
Neway; Gloria Lane (Secretary), Maria Marlo (Foreign Woman) and David Aiken (Mr. Kofner); Neway
and a man in a corridor; Norman Kelley (Magician)
and the Secretary; and the Secretary and five of the
characters waiting in the consulate.

Patak, L. Das Orchester, XVI (October, 1968), 441.
Review of the opera in Israel. It is a great success. One paragraph.

Pestalozza, Luigi. "Delude a Milano 'il Console' di Menotti."
Diapason (Milan), II (1951), 20-22.
Critical commentary. THE CONSUL at La Scala.

This is Menotti's most ambitious creation. He
aims to combine a theater of modern drama with
"classical beauty. " THE TELEPHONE and THE
MEDIUM realize this goal partly. THE MEDIUM
succeeds in holding the attention. But THE CON-
SUL is not a definitive drama and it is devoid of
the hope in his earlier operas. It shows the definite
limits in his methods. Its dramatic value is little
and the characters are not well realized. The
music and the action do not make an expressive
whole. For contemporary problems there is an
older styled music. Menotti's method of writing
text and music together is closer to cinematic
writing. But Menotti is unable to transform his
schemes into a language that is vitally modern.
His methods could have more effect if he used the
techniques of verismo for narration. Pestalozza
comments on THE TELEPHONE in the final paragraph. Six long paragraphs.

Phelan, Kappo. " 'The Consul' " Commonweal, LI (April 7,
    1950), 677.
        Analysis. Phelan approves of the term music-drama
        for the opera. He says Menotti has used a well-
        known story line and notes how Menotti imposes art
        on simple stage devices. Magda's big aria is bound
        to arouse the public. The third act is not consid-
        ered effective in comparison to the earlier ones.

Politzer, Heinz. Commentary, IX (May, 1950), 472-474.
        Criticism. Despite THE CONSUL's success it is
        radically different from the usual opera. Given its
        subject, Menotti has not done enough musically to
        explore elements in an original American form of
        opera. The story has some elements of a senti-
        mental "tear-jerker. " His music reminds this
        writer of Mascagni verismo. In the Magician epi-
        sode Menotti creates "theatre of magic. " Politzer
        praises the performance. Brief plot summary.

"Red Tape. " Time, LV (March 27, 1950), 42.
        Review. The writer points out that the idea comes
        from a refugee suicide story Menotti read. The
        pathos is almost constant. The score is called
        "distinctive. " Patricia Neway becomes a new star
        in what may be her biggest success. Photo of
        Neway, Marie Powers, Leon Lishner and Menotti.

Reich, Willi.   "Die Europaische Erstauffuhrung in Basel. "
    Melos, XVIII (February, 1951), 53-54.
          Review.   Reich claims it has a larger following in
          Basel than in New York because of its relevance to
          the Middle European.   He acclaims the characteri-
          zations and Inge Borkh's Magda.   Four paragraphs.
          Photo of Inge Borkh (Magda) and Else Boettcher
          (Secretary).

Sabin, Robert.   "Menotti's 'The Consul' Begins New York Run
    on Broadway. "   Musical America, LXX (March, 1950),
    7.
          Well written review of the Broadway production.
          Sabin gives a good plot telling.   Then he turns to
          the production and analyzes more briefly the music,
          the organization of scenes and the cast which he
          praises.   Photo of Patricia Neway and Marie
          Powers.

"Sadler's Wells. "   Opera, VII (March, 1956), 187-188.
          Review.   The critic first comments on the earlier
          reviews by Lincoln Kirstein and another critic who
          discussed The Cambridge and Sadler's Wells pro-
          ductions.   Like H. D. R. this critic does not admire
          the music or text.   It retains its timeliness, but it
          is not opera but musical theatre.   Amy Shuard
          (Magda) and Anna Pollak (Secretary) are excellent.
          All of the cast is effective.

"Sadler's Wells Opera. "   Musical Opinion, LXXVIII, (January,
    1955), 203.
          Review of a Sadler's Wells production.   The critic
          thinks the term, "music drama, " is wrong for this
          "thriller. "   A second hearing does not make it
          seem better.   Either as music alone or as a play
          without music it is weak.   This is a fine produc-
          tion.   Excellent performances are given by Amy
          Shuard (Magda), Anna Pollak (Secretary) and the re-
          mainder of the cast perform admirably.   Two large
          paragraphs.

"Sadler's Wells Opera. "   Opera, VI (January, 1955), 6.

Sahl, Hans.   "Berichte aus dem Ausland: Urauffuhrung in
    New York. "   Melos, XVII (?), (May, 1950), 152-153.
          Review of the first New York production.   Sahl is
          critical of the "tear-jerking" atmosphere.   He doubts

it will rank near Hindemith or Britten although he
feels it has craftsmanship for a modern work.
Four paragraphs.

Sandberg, Ingrid. "Menotti's 'The Consul' Given First
    Swedish Production. " Musical America, LXXII (July,
    1952), 12.
        Review of the Stockholm Opera production. One
        paragraph. Photos: Hugo Hasslo as John Sorel and
        Gertrud Wettergren as the Mother.

Sargeant, Winthrop, "Imperishable Menotti. " New Yorker,
    XXXVI (February 27, 1960), 133-135.
        Review of THE CONSUL which Sargeant rates his
        most tragic and strongest opera. Patricia Neway
        is a great success again as Magda. Two para-
        graphs. See also GENERAL.

Shawe-Taylor, Desmond. New Statesman and Nation, XLI
    (February 17, 1951), 183-184.
        Review. Shawe-Taylor says that musically the work
        might not be ranked too highly. It has hints of
        Puccini, Mussorgsky, Richard Strauss, Wolf-Fer-
        rari, the American ballad and film and radio music.
        The "home" scenes need a stronger musical defini-
        tion for the villain, the police agent. What Menotti
        achieves with the consulate scenes make the work
        memorable. The critic admires much of the fantasy
        and the contrast between the Magician's conjuring
        and Magda's aria although he finds the finale flat.

Singer, Samuel L. "Philadelphia Premieres Menotti's 'The
    Consul. ' " Musical Courier, CXLI (March 15, 1950),
    3.
        Review. Six short paragraphs. Photo of Magda and
        the Secretary.

Smith, Cecil. "Gian-Carlo Menotti: 'The Consul. ' " Music
    Library Association Notes, VIII (December, 1950), 125-
    126.
        Perceptive analysis. THE CONSUL breaks the
        Broadway record for a serious musical piece. If a
        work is a great commercial success, criticism of
        it must be approached "dually. " One approach must
        be to look at "artistic merit. " Menotti achieves
        more rapport with his libretto than musically. The
        popular audience should relate easily to all of the

music. Smith thinks of the opera as a "pastiche"
rather than as a masterly whole. He uses melodies
for content worthy of mere recitative or as arioso
with the orchestra carrying the main melody. Much
of the orchestra is for dependent roles such as
sound effects. To Smith AMELIA is still his finest
work.

Smith, Cecil. "Menotti's 'The Consul' Issued in Vocal
   Score. " Musical America, LXX (December 15, 1950),
   34-35.
      Analysis. Smith says Menotti is weak in developing
      characterization through individualized music. He
      has overlooked certain "central issues" in writing
      opera.

"Spoleto: Political Storm in a Tea-cup. " Opera, XXIII
   (March, 1972), 217.
      Paragraph about Menotti's letter in L'Unita in re-
      sponse to attacks by the communist press and Luigi
      Nono on the direction of the Florence Festival for
      allowing THE CONSUL as part of the festival.
      Quotes from Nono, L'Unita and the Rome corres-
      pondent of The Guardian.

Stuart, Charles. "Menotti and Mr. Smith. " Halle (Man-
   chester), XLVI (?), (April, 1951), 11-14.
      Review that has the opposite viewpoint of Caryl
      Brahm's in the same issue. Menotti strives to
      please Mr. Smith, the lay public, just as did Puc-
      cini. Stuart claims there is not a Puccini-derived
      note in the score. The style of the harmony could
      be Roussel or Respighi or many others, but it is
      economical. Stuart quotes the orchestra music for
      the Secret Police Agent to show Menotti's knack in
      establishing character quickly. The impishness of
      the woodwinds lends contrast to darker orchestral
      colors. The quoted orchestral music describing the
      consular office is again lightweight for a serious
      situation. The Sorel's tragedy does not fill THE
      CONSUL until the last act. Menotti's "incidental"
      music comes off better than the grander set pieces
      like the quintet. The third musical quotation illus-
      trates a "remote, aerial romanticism. " The re-
      viewer agrees that the weakest music is in the final
      scene. What goes before is "splendid. " Photo of
      Marie Powers (Mother) and Patricia Neway (Magda.).

Ter-Simonyan, M. "Here for the First Time. " Sovetskaia
    Muzyka, XXX (December, 1966), 74-77.
        Review of the first Russian CONSUL at the Ere-
        vansky Theatre.   In this work there is the theme
        of the "little man's" cruel treatment by the "capital-
        istic world. "   The music is traditional.   Stylistically
        the opera reminds one of Puccini.   The melodies
        are in the Italian vein with great emotion.   This is
        a good production.   Conductor A. Katanian succeeds
        in making the score support the varied mental
        states.   B. Afeyan, the director, emphasizes inner
        details of the roles in his interpretation rather than
        playing on the audience's emotions.   M. Mikhailow,
        the "scenographer, " also looks to the score to
        avoid unnecessary props.   His use of movie projec-
        tion is effective.   Magda is sung by A. Arutiunian
        and E. Mikadian.   Arutiunian convinces this critic
        more.   M. Chmashkian is more successful dramat-
        ically than vocally as the Secretary.   In A. Stepan-
        ian's efforts with the same role the voice is more
        effective.   Even secondary characters convey the
        tragic situation.   This critic wants an improvement
        in diction.   "A great artistic accomplishment. "
        Photo of the production.

Trevin, J. C.   "The World of the Theatre. "   Illustrated
    London News, CCXVIII (March 3, 1951), 346.
        One paragraph review of the excitement over the
        opera in London.   Photo of the fainted Magda
        (Neway) after seeing the Police Agent (Leon Lish-
        ner) as the Secretary (Gloria Lane) and two other
        women watch.

Ulanov, Barry.   "'The Consul. '"   Metronome, LXVI (May,
    1950), 12, 14.
        Review.   Ulanov praises Menotti for tackling this
        tale of oppression, but he calls the music "Puccini
        without memorable melody. "   Magda's climactic out-
        burst in the second act is the best moment.   The
        dream sequences show a mastery of the macabre
        although the second episode is less effective.   Photo
        of Gloria Lane (Secretary) chatting on the phone
        while Neway (Magda) waits.

"Uspesne Finale Sezony. "   Slovenska Hudba, X (n. 10, 1966),
    466-467.
        Review of THE CONSUL at Bratislava.   Four

paragraphs.

Vajda, Igor. "Opet Menotti Tentokrat Komicky. " Hudebni
    Rozhledy, XX (n. 15, 1967), 467.
    Review.

Watmough, David. Opera, XV (August, 1964), 548-549.
    Review of a Vancouver production. One paragraph.
    Photo of Chester Ludgin (John Sorel), Margarita
    Zambrana (Magda Sorel) and Dorothy Cole (Mother).

Watts, Douglas. " 'The Consul. ' " New Yorker, XXVI
    (March 25, 1950), 54, 56.
    Excellent review of the production at the Ethel
    Barrymore Theatre. Thorough summary of the
    plot. Watts considers Menotti's great talent to be
    relating musico-dramatic ideas for a rare unity.

Watts, Douglas. New Yorker, XXVIII (December 18, 1952),
    149.
    Review of the City Center production. The pro-
    duction is a reproduction of the Broadway one.
    Watts thinks certain weaknesses may be part of the
    opera rather than the production. He notes a cer-
    tain taste for the "bizarre. " The revival is not
    praised for its drama.

Weaver, William. "Florence. " Opera, XXIII (Autumn Fes-
    tival Issue, 1972), 113.
    Review of the production given at Florence and
    Spoleto staged by Menotti. It is a great success.
    Giovanna Fioroni is the Mother. One paragraph.
    Photo of THE CONSUL at Spoleto with Virginia
    Zeani as Magda.

Weaver, William. High Fidelity and Musical America, XXIII
    (October, 1972), MA29.
    Review of the production given at the Maggio Musi-
    cale and Spoleto. At Florence it is a success with
    Virginia Zeani as Magda, Joy Davidson the Secre-
    tary and Thomas Schippers conducting, Menotti stage
    director. One paragraph.

Wyatt, Euphemia Van Rensselaer. Catholic World, CLXXI
    (May, 1950), 148.
    Review. Wyatt admires the way Menotti combines
    speech and song faithful to the dramatic situation.

She is struck by the great suffering in the story.
The cast is praised.

THE DEATH OF THE BISHOP OF BRINDISI

Bell, Eleanor.   "Bravos for 'The Bishop.'"   Musical
    America, LXXXIII (July, 1963), 12.
        Review of the premiere of the dramatic cantata
        May 18, 1963, at the Cincinnati May Festival. The
        audience gives Menotti several curtain calls in its
        enthusiasm.   The cantata is for children's chorus,
        two soloists and orchestra.   It was commissioned
        by the Cincinnati May Festival Association. Menotti
        is overwhelmed by the audience's excitement.
        Richard Cross sings the Bishop, Rosalind Elias the
        Nun.   The story is about a Bishop who "berates"
        himself for having permitted the Children's Crusade.
        Bell quotes several lines for the Bishop and the
        chorus.   The climax is poignant.   Menotti requests
        that the final chorus be sung at his funeral.

"Boston Symphony."   Musical America, LXXXIV (December,
    1964), 119-120.
        Review of the premiere New York performance in
        Philharmonic Hall performed by the Boston Sym-
        phony.   The reviewer finds the music uninspiring,
        unoriginal and sometimes banal.   He suggests
        Menotti look to Britten for his music for children.
        The critic also lashes out at the libretto.   The per-
        formance does justice to the work.   George London
        as the Bishop and Lili Chookasian as the Nun are
        joined by the New England Conservatory Chorus and
        the Catholic Memorial and St. Joseph's High School
        Glee Clubs.   Plot summary.

Felton, James.   "Temple Festival Gets a Roof Over Its Head."
    High Fidelity/Musical America, XXI (November, 1971),
    MA 19, 22.
        Review of the world premiere of the staged version
        of THE DEATH.   Felton does not think the drama
        of the work merits an attempted change to opera.
        At times there is a "montage of disconnected cha-
        rades rather than a compelling dramatic unity."
        Photo of Menotti listening to THE DEATH.   See also
        THE MEDIUM.

Jacobs, Arthur. "Ambler, Pennsylvania. " Musical Times,
    CXII (September, 1971), 889.
        One paragraph review of THE DEATH, its first
        staging at the Temple University Music Festival and
        Institute. Jacobs says it is a cantata, not an opera
        and not one of Menotti's stronger works. See also
        THE MEDIUM.

Kessler, Hansi. "Ballett. Konzert. " Musica, XX (n. 1,
    1966), 24.
        Brief review. Although the orchestration is sin-
        cerely done, it falls back on "safe" devices in
        sacred music. The conductor Jerzy Semkov, solo-
        ists Edgar Diaz (first name may be Justino) and
        Carol Smith and the choruses help make the per-
        formance a success.

Luten, C. J. "Menotti: 'The Death of the Bishop of Brin-
    disi. ' " Opera News, XXIX (April 3, 1965), 34.
        Review of the RCA Victor recording. Luten calls
        it an excellent recording. The score does not
        always hold the attention. The Boston Symphony
        plays beautifully and George London and Lili Chook-
        asian are the soloists.

"Mailand. " Musik und Gesellschaft, XVI (March, 1966), 200-
    201.
        Short review and analysis of the first Italian per-
        formance. THE DEATH is not an opera. It is not
        remarkable for musical ideas. Menotti's story con-
        tent comes from the Story of the Crusades by
        Adolph Waas. Justino Diaz is the Bishop, Carol
        Smith the Nun (names may be misspelled?) The
        Italian translation is sometimes awkward. The
        choruses from La Scala and Prague are under
        Marketa Kursova's direction. The audience warmly
        applauds. Plot summary.

Rogers, Harold. "Massachusetts With Little Emotion. "
    Musical America, LXXXIV (December, 1964), 63.
        Review of the premiere Boston performance con-
        ducted by Erich Leinsdorf. He is an excellent in-
        terpreter of the "oratorio. " He brings unusual
        commitment to the Menotti work. It is sung by
        New England Conservatory Chorus, George London
        (Bishop) and Lili Chookasian (Nun). Both soloists
        are moving. Menotti has produced an excellent score,
        "his most ingratiating. "

Sargeant, Winthrop. New Yorker, XL (October 31, 1964), 23.
    Review of the New York premiere performance.
    Sargeant finds the work sincere, at other times
    more theatrical. THE DEATH poses a familiar
    Menotti dilemma of real or imagined guilt. Sargeant
    rates it as one of Menotti's most powerful works, a
    beautiful blending of words and music.

Saturday Review, XLVII (November 7, 1964), 28.
    Review of the New York performance in Philhar-
    monic Hall. THE DEATH illustrates Menotti's gifts
    in harmony. He uses simple means for an unsimple
    psychological subject. This simplicity of means
    works well only in parts; it needs more variety in
    expression. All of the performers are effective;
    the choruses are brilliant. Four paragraphs.

HELP! HELP! THE GLOBOLINKS [Hilfe! Hilfe! die Globo-
links]

Ardoin, John. "Santa Fe - Five Operas in Four Days."
    Opera, XX (November, 1969), 977-978.
    Review of the first American performance at the
    Santa Fe Opera. Two short paragraphs.

Bellingardi, Luigi. "Rome." Opera, XXIII (June, 1972), 552.
    Brief review at the Teatro Dell'Opera in Rome. It
    is a sizable success. Singers are mentioned for
    Emily and Mme. Euterpova. See also AMAHL.

Bloomfield, T. "Switzerland: Menotti Revival." Opera,
    XXIII (March, 1972), 269.
    See also AMAHL.

Dannenberg, Peter. "Auftrags Kompositionen fur Kinder."
    Neue Musikzeitung, XVIII (February-March, 1969), 7.
    Commentary. This is not wholly composed as a
    contemporary work nor as a cliche. Its main appeal
    is for older children. The special effects give the
    work a fascinating performance.

Geitel, Klaus. "Hamburg: Wer Hat Angst vor Globolinks?"
    Das Orchester, XVII (March, 1969), 111.
    Review of the Hamburg production. Menotti is
    grateful to Rolf Liebermann, Nicolas Schoeffer and
    Alwin Nikolais for their collaboration on HELP!,

aiding in its laughable success. Schoeffer has
created unusual structures of colored lights in mo-
tion projected on a screen. Nikolais is responsible
for the "fantastic" movements. The Hamburg ap-
plauds much during the scenes. Geitel describes
the Globolinks. Arlene Saunders excites them as
Madame Euterpova, the music teacher. Even though
it is difficult to tell how far Menotti is from the
mainstream of modern music, he has succeeded in
writing an opera for children. Edith Mathis does
well as Emily in a "boyish soprano." His music
for the characters does not make much effect.
Geitel notes some Stravinsky and Puccini traces.
Matthias Kuntzsch conducts. The cast wins much
applause. Their work answers well the argument
that Menotti's works are not progressive. Photo of
Dr. Stone (Raymond Wolansky) and the Globolinks.
Plot highlights. See also AMAHL.

_____. "Wer Hat Angst vor Globolinks?" Neue Zeits-
chrift fur Musik, CXXX (February, 1969), 54-55.
Review of the Hamburg State Opera production.
Photo of Raymond Wolansky as Dr. Stone blind-
folded with the Globolinks.

Joachim, Heinz. "Hamburg." Opera, XX (March, 1969),
236-237.
Review of HELP! at the Hamburg State Opera.
Menotti stages both operas. Photos: Five characters in the library and Edith Mathis (Emily) and
William Workman (Tony) facing the Globolinks. See
also AMAHL.

Kupferberg, Herbert. "Bleeps in the Night." Life, LXI
(December 19, 1969), 14.
Review of the New York City Opera production.
Kupferberg feels the opera is very enjoyable. He
points to Menotti's success with the public, if not
the critics. In this parable he says Menotti is
commenting on contemporary mechanization. The
story leads to the point that music or art is more
emotional than intellectual. The opera entertains
the young. Photo of three Globolinks floating
around a school bus.

"Magic and the Globolinks." Time, XCI (January 3, 1969),
50.

Review of the world premiere at the Hamburg State
Opera. HELP! is intended as "total theater."
Menotti is aided by kinetic sculptor Nicholas Schoeffer and choreographer Alwin Nikolais.   In the
opera there is a meeting of the mechanized music
generation. Brief plot summary. Photo of the
Globolinks and the school bus.

Marks, Marcis. Dance Magazine. XLIV (March, 1970), 86.
Review of HELP! at the City Center. Marks is
disappointed with the opera. She feels Nikolais'
work is not his best. The electronic score has
more appeal for children than the usual singing.
Movements for the Globolinks are unimaginative.
Possibilities to exploit foolish situations are not
realized adequately. The cast is effective. See
also AMAHL.

Merkling, Frank. Opera News, XXXIV (September 20, 1969),
23.
Review of HELP! at the Santa Fe Opera.

Rizzo, Francis. "Globolinks' Friend." Opera News, XXXIV
(December 20, 1969), 17.
Article about the connection between HELP! and
choreographer Alwin Nikolais. Menotti has the
choreographer in mind when he composes HELP!
The Globolinks are associated with creatures in
Nikolais' Allegory. Menotti uses Nikolais' sound
studio as motivation for the opera's electronic music.
Nikolais has difficulties integrating the dancers with
Schoeffer's settings.

Rouse, Jack. "I Believe in Globolinks." Music Journal,
XXVIII (April, 1970), 30-31.
Interesting article about the opera in a production
at College-Conservatory of Music at the University
of Cincinnati. Rouse is the stage director. He
sees the work as a brief look at the world through
a child's eyes. He found his cast unfamiliar with
the opera, unusual in educational opera theatre. He
discusses the characters, their charm. The production must be slick and imaginative. There are
good opportunities for young acting singers. The
opera is basically fun.

Schneiders, Heinz-Ludwig. "Musikalisches Sacharin." Opern

Welt, IV (April, 1971), 41.
    Review of the Hamburg production. His style is
    diverse. Menotti's statement about the opera's not
    being avant-garde is not wholly true. With produc-
    tion and cast credits. Five paragraphs.

Schonberg, Harold C. "Did Menotti Beat 'The Devils'?"
    Opera Journal, II (n. 4, 1969), 34-35.
    Harold Schonberg's review in the New York Times,
    August 24.

_____. "Menotti's Globolinks Invade Santa Fe." Opera
    Journal, II (n. 4, 1969), 33-34.
    Reprint of Schonberg's review of HELP! in the New
    York Times August 18 of the Santa Fe production.

Smith, Patrick J. "Penderecki & Menotti: Pros and Cons."
    High Fidelity/Musical America, MA, XIX (November,
    1969), 24-25+.
    Review of the Santa Fe Opera Production. It is a
    success. Smith says the work is saved by the
    charm of the Globolinks and the sounds describing
    them. The libretto is not praised. Photo of the
    Globolinks attacking the school bus.

Sutcliffe, James Helme. "Hamburg." Opera News, XXXIII
    (February 8, 1969), 32-33.
    Review of the opera at Hamburg. Over a column.
    Photos of the Globolinks stopping the school bus and
    Arlene Saunders (Mme. Euterpova) giving a lecture
    to five other characters.

_____. High Fidelity/Musical America, MA, XIX (April,
    1969), 27-28.
    Review of the world premiere at Hamburg. Sutcliffe
    is enthusiastic. With plot summary. Photo of Glo-
    bolinks attacking the school bus. See also AMAHL.

Wagner, K. "Kaviar fuers Kindervolk...." Melos, XXXVI
    (February, 1969), 79-81.
    Review of the Hamburg production. HELP! is a
    Christmas premiere work. Photos: Globolink and
    the light structures and Edith Mathis (Emily) and
    William Workman (Tony) to the side of the school
    bus. See also AMAHL.

Weinstock, Herbert. Opera, XXI (March, 1970), 223-224.

Review of first New York performance of HELP! at
the City Center Theatre on a double bill. Weinstock says the opera adds nothing to operatic literature. See also AMAHL.

Worbs, Hans Christoph. "Eine Neue Kinderoper von Menotti."
Schwerzerische Musikzietung, CIX (n. 1, 1969), 36.
Review of the Hamburg production. Both young and
old are charmed by this mixture of sound and sight.
Three paragraphs.

_____. "Menotti's Neue Kinderoper. " Musica, XXIII
(April, 1969), 148-149.
Review of the new opera at Hamburg's Staatsoper.
Photo of Edith Mathis and William Workman facing
the Globolinks.

Zytowski, C. B. Opera Journal, III (n. 1, 1970), 23-25.
Review of HELP! at the Santa Fe Opera. The reviewer concludes that the opera may be performed
for a time.

THE ISLAND GOD

Barlow, L. M. "In the Theatre. " Modern Music, XIX,
(March-April, 1942), 196-197.
Review of THE ISLAND GOD, the world premiere
at the Metropolitan Opera. THE ISLAND GOD is
grand philosophical opera that has little action. It
is universal and unspecific and the characters emerge
as types. This story of man creating God in His
own likeness lacks a grandeur that it needs. Barlow criticizes the poor English diction although he
praises the singing.

San Francisco Symphony Program Notes, (January 3, 1957),
197-201.
Mostly Menotti's comments. He says it was an
"important experiment, and a point of departure. "
He wanted to get away from the formulas of
AMELIA and THE OLD MAID. The subject is the
relationship between reality and faith. He explains
the story. The situation of the First and Second
Interludes is described.

Peiper, Herbert F. Musical Courier, CXXV (February 20,

1942), 3.
Excellent review of the opera which has its world
premiere at the Metropolitan Opera February 20,
the second of a double bill with Pagliacci. The reviewer feels the work is deadly theater while ad-
mitting the young Menotti's talents. More than
adequate treatment of the plot.

LABYRINTH

Ardoin, John. "Menotti's 'Labyrinth.'" Opera News,
    LXXXIII (April, 1963), 53.
        Review of the NBC Opera television premiere
        March 5. Short plot summary. Ardoin thinks the
        opera contains many melodic patterns that Menotti
        has used earlier. The opera is perhaps a regres-
        sion for him. The cast is praised.

Breuer, Robert. "Menotti's Weg ins Freie uber den Ameri-
    kanischen Bildschirm." Melos, XXX (April, 1963),
    133-134.
        Review. LABYRINTH is unusual since it is an
        operatic riddle. Menotti uses symbolic meanings.
        NBC's opera company performs well and there are
        no weak performances from principals. It is simple
        music for radical ideas.

Haggin, B. H. Hudson Review, XVI (Autumn, 1963), 437.
        Brief review that is savagely critical and negative.
        One paragraph.

Kolodin, Irving. "Menotti's 'Labyrinth.'" Saturday Review,
    XLVI (March 16, 1963), 94.
        Review of the first performance of this television
        opera. Kolodin finds the work very imaginative in
        its planning for television. Menotti may be saying
        in this work that death is not life's end.

"Like a Self-Caricature." Opera, XIV (June, 1963), 393-394.
        Review. LABYRINTH is a disappointment. This
        reviewer thinks the libretto and music are inferior.
        Brief plot summary. Four short paragraphs.
        Photos: Bride and Groom (Judith Raskin and John
        Reardon) encounter the Old Man (Robert White); a
        flooded railway car with John Reardon in the center.

"Menotti's Hour. " Time, LXXXI (March 8, 1963), 46.
    Review. LABYRINTH is totally for television; its
    tricks could not be duplicated on stage. There are
    such video devices as a "gravity-free tea party
    aboard a rocket. " If characters and mood have not
    been developed, the music does show skill. Menotti
    has striven to be "unoperatic. " Plot summary.
    Photos: John Reardon (Groom) in a rocket and with
    swimmers in a water-filled railroad day coach.

Prideaux, Tom. "Menotti's Opera Runs Riot With a Flood of
    Tricks. " Life, LIV (March 8, 1963), 46.
    Entertaining article. Photos of Menotti directing a
    "baffled" singer and a flooded railroad car with the
    passengers fishing or playing water sports.

Reisfeld, Bert. "Menotti's 'Labyrinth. ' " Musica, XVII
    (May-June, 1963), 125.
    Review. Again the libretto impresses one more
    than the music. This is good television music. As
    television opera AMAHL is a superior example. The
    cast of John Reardon, Judith Raskin, Elaine Bonazzi,
    Robert White, Beverly Wolff and Frank Poretta is
    excellent. Plot summary. Over one column.

Sargeant, Winthrop. "Menotti's New One. " New Yorker,
    XXXIX (March 9, 1963), 148-149.
    Review of LABYRINTH on NBC-TV Opera. Sargeant
    views the work as an entertaining fantasy. He dis-
    cusses the stagework and music with insight. Al-
    though it is not a major work, it works well for a
    short forty minutes.

THE LAST SAVAGE [Le Dernier Sauvage]

"A Banal Savage. " Time, LXXXIII (January 31, 1964), 33.
    Article about the uneven career of THE LAST
    SAVAGE. It is crucified by the French critics.
    This writer considers it unsuccessful at the Metro-
    politan. It is basically commonplace. The music
    with a few exceptions does not live up to Menotti's
    reputation. One excuse might be the poor English
    translation. Another could be Menotti's naivete for
    comedy. Plot summary in Timese. Photo of George
    London (title role) and Roberta Peters (Kitty).

Bernheimer, Martin. "Returning Savage. " Saturday Review,
     XLVIII (January 16, 1965), 22.
          Review at the Metropolitan Opera.   Robert La
          Marchina is the new conductor.   Two paragraphs.

Bowen, Jean. "Menotti's 'The Last Savage. ' "   Listen, I
     (March-April, 1964), 21-22.
          Review of the Metropolitan Opera production.   Miss
          Bowen congratulates the Metropolitan on a brilliant
          production for a work that is short of excellent
          music.   Unlike the Barber of Seville, it has weak
          music.   She disagrees with his attitude toward
          opera buffa, for she says comic opera can be writ-
          ten in a difficult musical style as is Britten's A
          Midsummer Night's Dream.   Photo of Act I in the
          Metropolitan production.

Breuer, R. "Mit Menotti Zuruck Natur. "   Melos, XXXI
     (April, 1964), 134-135.
          Review of the Metropolitan Opera production.   Four
          paragraphs.   Photos: the caged George London (title
          role) in front of the maharajah's palace; the cock-
          tail party scene.

Brozen, Michael. "Quote Un Quote. "   Musical America,
     LXXXIV (January, 1964), 28.
          Menotti discusses THE LAST SAVAGE.   There have
          been problems with the opera's title.   Also men-
          tioned are the switch to the Opera-Comique in
          Paris, the Italian text and translation, the stock
          figures used for characters, Montresor's sets and
          Menotti's musical style.   Photo of the composer.

"'Le Dernier Sauvage. ' "   World Premieres, XV (December,
     1963), 43.
          Listing of the world premiere at the Opera-Comique
          with excerpts from reviews by Rene Dumesnil in
          Le Monde, Claude Samuel in Paris-Presse, Claren-
          don in Le Figaro, Marcel Landowski in L'Informa-
          tion Humanite and J. Bourgeois in Arts.

Fitzgerald, Gerald. "Cast of the Characters. "   Opera News,
     XXVIII (February 8, 1964), 13-15.
          Seven singers in the Metropolitan Opera production
          discuss their roles.   The singers are: Roberta
          Peters, coloratura (Kitty); Morley Meredith, bass-
          baritone (Mr. Scattergood); Lili Chookasian, con-

tralto (Majaranee); Ezio Flagello, bass (Majarajah);
Teresa Stratas, soprano (Sardula); Nicolai Gedda,
tenor; and George London, bass-baritone (Abdul, the
title role).   Fourteen photos of the composer, rehearsal scenes and individual singers.

Freeman, John W.   "Idyllic Retreat. " Opera News, XXVIII
(February 8, 1964), 24-25.
Perceptive analysis of THE LAST SAVAGE.   The
singing style is fancier than usual for him.   Musical
quotations from the roles of the Maharajah, Scatter-
good, Kitty, the Composer, Sardula, Abdul, two
orchestral quotations and a "tag theme. "

Golea, Antoine.   "Les Caprices d'Euterpe. " Musica (Chaix),
XCVII (December, 1963), 41.
Review article.   Golea charges that THE CONSUL
and THE MEDIUM fooled discriminating people about
their worth.   The excellent production, conducting
and stage direction did not mask the "emptiness" of
THE LAST SAVAGE.   Golea says a sometimes funny
story is negated by the music and text.   This
"operetta" does not belong at the Opera-Comique.
Brief plot summary.

Harrison, Jay S.   Musical America, LXXXIV (February,
1964), 25-26.
Review of the American premiere of THE LAST
SAVAGE at the Metropolitan Opera.   Harrison says
the opera doesn't work as theater.   The plot is old-
fashioned and the translation is very awkward.   He
calls the score "derivative. "   But he praises the
production and singing.   Photos: a dress rehearsal
break and the Act I finale, George London as the
caged savage.

Helm, E.   "Eine Eintonige Saison. " Neue Zeitschrift fur
Musik, CXXV (n. 5, 1964), 209.
Short review notice of the Metropolitan production.
Photo of Kitty's apartment in Act II, the Last
Savage (George London) rejecting Western clothes.
Others in the group are the designers played by
Paul Franke, Norman Scott, Andrea Velis and
Roberta Peters (Kitty).

"L'Homme Sauvage. " Musica (Chaix), XCVII (December,
1963), 11.

Article. Finally the opera's title came from a
literal translation of the English rather than The
Savage Man. Menotti is unfamiliar with French
rehearsal time. Then he realizes that the choruses
and the principals do not rehearse at the same
place and that there are union problems. Menotti
is irritated when some complain of overwork. Eight
very short paragraphs.

Jacobs, Arthur. "Menotti in Paris." Opera, XIV (Decem-
    ber, 1963), 803-804.
    Review. This opera may be more suitable for a
    smaller house than the Metropolitan Opera. The
    first public performance is warmly received at the
    Opera-Comique. Musically this is an attempted
    revival of comic opera reminiscent of Cimarosa and
    Puccini. It is lacking in unity. For Frenchness,
    there is a solo for the caged savage of considerable
    charm and the Indian setting. The performance is
    a great success with good singing. Plot summary.

Kaufman, Wolfe. "Menotti's 'Last Savage.'" Variety,
    CCXXXII (November 6, 1963), 55+.
    Review of the Metropolitan production. Kaufman
    states Menotti risks a great deal by trying for a
    successful comic opera. Italian might be more
    suitable than English. More than anything else the
    music entertains, for this is an opera about operatic
    conventions. Menotti composes this directly to his
    audience, not over or under their intelligence. His
    inventiveness sometimes falls short. Plot summary.

"'The Last Savage.'" Life, LVI (February 14, 1964), 66A-
    66B.
    Article of two paragraphs. Photos: full page of
    caged George London in a rage at his cage-bearers;
    Roberta Peters (Kitty) introducing the savage to
    Western lovemaking; Kitty with her father (Morley
    Meredith).

"'The Last Savage.'" Opera News, XXVIII (February 8,
    1964), 17-23.
    Insert for the Saturday matinee Metropolitan Opera
    broadcast of THE SAVAGE. The first page is the
    playbill for the world premiere in Paris. On the
    second page is the story with musical numbers in-
    dicated with the libretto page. "The Background"

is on the next page with four drawings of the stage
setting.   The next page has photographs of the
major cast members and approximate timings for
the radio broadcasts.   A full page photograph plus
three Montresor drawings and six photographs of the
Metropolitan make up the next three pages.

"Letter from Paris. " New Yorker, XXXIX (November 2,
    1963), 198, 200.
        Review of the world premiere at the Opera-Comique.
        Very good plot summary.   The audience's reactions
        are much more favorable than the critic's.   This
        writer feels the critics are too negative.

Mayer, Martin.   "'Savage' by Marchina. "   High Fidelity/
    Musical America, XV (March, 1965), 86F.
        Review at the Metropolitan.   It is led by a new
        conductor, Robert LaMarchina.   Mayer sees the
        opera as trivial and disapproves of some of the
        staging.

"Menotti's Eleventh. "   Newsweek, LXIII (February 3, 1964),
    77.
        Review of the Metropolitan production.   Menotti may
        be a favorite with the public but not with many
        critics.   Montresor's production is attractive and
        efficient.   The story is commonplace; the senti-
        mental music is a hit at the Met.   Plot summary.
        Photo of the caged savage in Act I with Morley
        Meredith (Mr. Scattergood) and Roberta Peters
        (Kitty).

Ohnen, Frank.   "Parijs. "   Mens en Melodie, XVIII (Decem-
    ber, 1963), 371-372.
        Review.   Blame for some of the opera's problems
        in Paris should fall on the Opera-Comique which
        usually gives smaller works.   Menotti's orchestra
        is too heavy for the Opera Comique's capacity. The
        first act reminds this critic of Meyerbeer or Halevy
        with its accent on the exotic and oriental.   The
        cocktail party scene brings out Menotti's knack for
        spectacle.   Laughter results more from the situa-
        tions than the composer's wit.   His music seems at
        home in the Donizetti and Puccini periods.   Mady
        Mesple (Kitty) and Gabriel Bacquier (Abdul) are
        praised.   Plot summary.

Opera News, XXVIII (October 19, 1963), 17.
Color page of Beni Montresor's drawing of an Indian courtyard for the Metropolitan Opera production.

"Opera Review." Variety, CCXXXIII (January 29, 1964), 70.
Review. It is a "hybrid" show. Much of satire is shaky material. Menotti's talents make it generally fun. The cleverness of the spoofs illustrate again his theatrical know-how. There are few set pieces to excite the listener. All in all it has attractive variety which offsets much possible harsh criticisms.

"Opera Review." Variety, CCXXXVII (January 13, 1965), 82.
Review at the Metropolitan Opera on New Year's Eve. The reviewer disapproves of the "effeminate" tailors. Menotti's intentions are questioned. George London does well in the title role.

Osborne, Conrad. Musical Times, CV (April, 1964), 284.
Osborne says the opera is very enjoyable. He admires Menotti's practical stagecraft. The Met production is a successful one. Photo of the Met production.

Pincherle, Marc. "Nel regno delle fate: 'L'Ultimo Selvaggio.'" Musica d'Oggi, VI (n. 6, 1963), 266-268.
Review of the Opera-Comique production. Georges Hirsch of the Paris Opera commissioned a large opera with exoticism. A shift to the Opera-Comique causes Menotti to make many changes. Public reaction is more favorable than the critic's. The translation makes a problem. The small stage of the house causes a "heavy" orchestral sound. Most enthusiasm goes to the Chicago scenes. The overture, compared to French operetta, may be too long, but it has the naturalness of the young Poulenc. Menotti's reaction to atonalism has exaggerated the score's "charm." Vigor is missing in arias of this work. While some of the humor fails, the ensembles are strong. There is an admirable concentration. Pincherle sees some resemblance to Mascagni's verismo. The performers are widely praised. Plot summary. Complete credits in a box.

Plussain, Michel. Music Journal, XXII (March, 1964), 117-118.
The opera buffa is complimented for its orchestra-

tion and music.   The production and cast are also
praised.

"Le Retour de Gian-Carlo Menotti. "   Musica (Chaix), XCIV
    (January, 1962), 13.
        Article.   The Paris Opera had commissioned it over
        a year ago.   Menotti's discussions in Paris lead to
        a new title, Abdul or The Last Superman.   Ernest
        Blanc who is to sing the title role asks to see the
        score.

Reynolds, Michael.   "The Abominable Savage. "   Music and
    Musicians, XII (January, 1964), 32.
        Review of the Opera-Comique production sung in
        French.   Reynolds finds little musical value in the
        work.   He praises both the cast and Andre Beaure-
        paire's sets and costumes.   Plot summary.   Seven
        paragraphs.

Sabin, Robert.   "Synthetic Savage. "   Opera, XV (April, 1964),
    241-242.
        Review of the Metropolitan Opera production.   Sabin
        calls the score "lifeless. "   George London and
        Roberta Peters are a success as the Savage and
        Kitty.   The cast is uniformly good.   Four para-
        graphs.   Photos: the caged savage (George London)
        in Act I and London and Roberta Peters in the
        Chicago scene.

"Sad Savage. "   Time, LXXXII (November 1, 1963), 63.
        Review about the world premiere.   The first para-
        graph is a plot summation.   The premiere is a dis-
        appointment.   The comic work was first commis-
        sioned for the Paris Opera.   Le Figaro is savagely
        critical.

Samuel, Claude.   "Les Metamorphoses d'un Sauvage. "   Le
    Guide du Concert et du Disque, CDXVI (February 15,
    1964), 8.
        Article.   Last fall Paris critics attacked the opera.
        Menotti reacts by asserting he dares to stand apart
        from the dissonance in fashion.   Samuel quotes
        Harold Schonberg of the New York Times who calls
        it a transplanted musical comedy.   In contrast, critic
        Alan Rich of the New York Herald Tribune finds it
        "amusing" and "delicious" and the Metropolitan's
        first audience is similarly delighted.   Samuel says

the Metropolitan Opera has "transformed" the opera.
Only Xavier Depraz is superior to his American
counterpart in the French cast. The Americans
have a great advantage in the orchestra led well by
Thomas Schippers. Whether in Paris or New York,
the objections are the same. Why should this be
given while the works of Prokofiev or Henze are
not? Rudolf Bing, the Met's manager, can be con-
soled by the fact it is part of a subscription series
that is selling well. Photos: Kitty and the Savage
at the Opera-Comique and a left profile of Menotti.

Sarnette, Eric. "'Le Dernier Sauvage.'" Musique et Radio,
      LIII (December, 1970), 373.
            Review of the Opera-Comique production. Menotti
            writes appropriate music for this farcical content.
            Critics have not received it well. Sarnette thinks
            it is praiseworthy. Photo of the Opera-Comique
            production with the caged savage.

Soria, Dorle J. "The First Savage." Opera News, XXVIII
      (December 7, 1963), 30-31.
            Article of the world premiere at the Opera-Comique.
            Much of this centers on the society audience. With
            some press reactions. Photo of the millionaire
            (Depraz), Kitty (Mesple) and the caged savage (Bac-
            quier).

Stein, Elliott. Musical Times, CX (January, 1964), 42.
            Review of the world premiere at the Opera-Comique.
            Stein is largely unenthusiastic; the French newspaper
            reviews show disgust over the work.

Ubel, Ruth. "Von der Metropolitan Oper." Musica, XVII
      (July-August, 1964), 209.
            Review. It is successful at the Metropolitan.
            Menotti is the stage director, Beni Montresor the
            designer and Thomas Schippers the conductor. An
            outstanding cast headed by George London apparently
            has as much fun as the audience. One paragraph.
            Photo of Menotti stage directing.

MARIA GOLOVIN

Barichella, Monique. "Paris." Opera Canada, XIII (n. 1,
      1972), 25.

Review of the revised opera, its Paris Opera premiere December 7, 1971. The house is largely
empty but receives the work warmly. The cast is
excellent as is the orchestra conducted by Reynald
Giovaninetti. Two paragraphs.

Bernstein, Bob. "TV 'Golovin' Can Spark LP Sales. " Billboard, LXXI (March 23, 1959), 24.
Brief review of the NBC-TV production March 8.

"Blind, Burning and Bland. " Time, LXXII (November 17,
1958), 54+.
Review of four paragraphs of MARIA at the Martin
Beck Theatre in New York. It is a "disappoint-
ment. " Photo of Menotti directing Franca Duval
(Maria) and Richard Cross (Donato).

Briner, A. "Gian-Carlo Menotti's Neue Oper 'Maria Golovin. ' " Schweizerische Musikzeitung, XCVIII (October,
1958), 379-380.

"Brussels. " Opera, IX (November, 1958), 712+.
Review of the August world premiere in Brussels.
The work has an impermanent quality. Menotti's
thrills are more satisfying than his music. Plot
summary. Photos: Herbert Handt (Dr. Zuckertanz),
Patricia Neway (Mother) and Franca Duval (Maria);
Neway plays the piano with Duval and Handt; Reuben
Ter-Arutanian's sketch for the living room set.

Castiglioni, V. La Scala, CX (January, 1959), 37.
Review of MARIA at La Scala. The cast includes
Clara Petrella as Maria, Mario Petri as Donato and
Adriana Lazzarini as the Mother. Photos: Menotti
with Petrella and Mario Petri and Lorenzo Muti in
a scene.

Chedorge, A. "L'Opera de Marseille le Theatre Moderne et
Louis Ducreux. " Opera (France), XI (n. 93, 1971),
10-12.
Cover illustrated and other illustrations.

Coleman, Emily. "Menotti, Very Momentarily. " Theatre
Arts, XLIII (January, 1959), 43.
Review. Coleman says calling MARIA a "musical
drama" fails this time. Coleman feels MARIA is
worthy of more than its five performances on

Broadway. She notes the "morbid" subject and
weak musical score. Three paragraphs. Photo of
Franca Duval (Maria), Ruth Kobart (Housekeeper)
and Richard Cross (Donato).

Dragadze, Peter. "La Scala Presents Lavish 'Turandot!' As
    Season Begins." Musical America, LXXIX (January 1,
    1959), 3.
        Review of MARIA at La Scala. Press reactions are
        varied. Menotti has casting problems in this pro-
        duction which is received with enthusiasm by the
        public.

Evett, Robert. "A Menotti 'Melodrama.'" New Republic,
    XXII (November 17, 1958), 22-23.
        Review. One can assume it is not ended despite its
        very short Broadway run. The music is not enough
        to divert from the action. MARIA's symbols are
        not realized because none of the characters arouses
        sympathy. The music which has a variety of styles
        helps. But he shows no originality in the music.
        He is a conservative composer without a personal
        musical style. Plot summary.

Eyer, Ronald. "Menotti's Latest Opera Brought to Broad-
    way." Musical America, LXXVIII (November 15,1958),
    18.
        Review. Eyer ponders when Menotti will "let go"
        lyrically. He calls the libretto "thin." The cast is
        praised.

Gambetta, Rosario. "Milan: Theatre de la Scala, Creation de
    'Maria Golovin' de Menotti." Le Guide du Concert et
    du Disque, XXXIX (January 9, 1959), 620.
        Review of the La Scala production. He shows us
        people who are self-imprisoned due to circumstances.
        The cast is excellent as are the direction and sets.
        MARIA is a success with eighteen curtain calls.
        Plot summary. Photo of Clara Petrella (Maria) and
        Mario Petri (Donato).

"I've Been Broke...." Newsweek, LII (November, 1958),
    75.
        Article about the failure of MARIA on Broadway.
        Quotes from Menotti on the quality of text and music.
        He calls them a "marriage." The writer thinks
        MARIA will not be forgotten. Photo of Menotti.

Johnson, David. High Fidelity, IX (April 1959), 63-64.
    Review of the RCA Victor recording. The critic is
    disappointed. He thinks the content is not sub-
    stantial for three acts. The original cast performs.
    Only Herbert Handt as Dr. Zuckertanz is fully
    praised. The orchestra is considered too small.
    Plot summary. Five paragraphs.

Klein, R. "'Maria Golovin' in Brussels Welturaufgefuhrt. "
    Oesterreichische Musikzeitschrift, XIII (September,
    1958), 391-392.

Kolodin, Irving. "Menotti's Mania. " Saturday Review, XLI
    (November 22, 1958), 43.
    Perceptive review of MARIA in its American pre-
    miere. Kolodin says Menotti has increased in
    musical resources while questioning other devices
    he uses.

"'Maria Golovin. '" Musical Courier, CLVIII (December,
    1958), 14.
    Well written review of MARIA GOLOVIN at the
    Martin Beck Theatre. This first U. S. hearing lasts
    only five nights. The reviewer attributes this to
    the plot and the music which is said to be less
    effective than earlier Menotti.

"'Maria Golovin. '" Variety, CCXII (November 12, 1958),
    58+.
    Review. MARIA is "pretty good" as entertainment.
    As a match between the drama and the music, the
    results are uneven. Character relationships are
    not strong despite a detailed plot. By the end the
    blind man is thoroughly unsympathetic. There is
    solid drama despite the blind man's self-pity. A
    trio for the Mother, a woman and the housemaid is
    effective. Franca Duval is almost the star as
    Maria. Symbolism is used with the mute son and
    the bird cages in the opening scene. Richard Cross
    is strong as the blind man.

" 'Maria Golovin. '" Variety, CCXIV (March 11, 1959), 37.
    Review of the NBC-TV production. MARIA perhaps
    should have been given on television first. The
    biggest problems are musical ones. Lyrical possi-
    bilities are not realized as the tragedy deepens.
    Ruth Kobart, Richard Cross, Franca Duval, Patricia

Neway are excellent.   Brief plot summary and complete credits.

" 'Maria Golovin.' "   Variety, CCXIV (April 8, 1959), 72.
Review of the New York City Opera production.
Some of the music is of excellent quality.   The pro-
duction is excellent.

Mayer, Tony.   "Menotti Revises 'Maria Golovin.' "   Opera,
XXII (June, 1971), 30.
Review of the revised MARIA in Marseilles on Jan-
uary 29.   Menotti seems "out of touch" with today's
opera.   This is a drama of jealousy.   The music
is old fashioned but effective; its "impact" is great.
The cast of Richard Stilwell, Suzanne Sarocca,
Denise Scharley, Daniele Grimax, and Francis
Dresse is excellent.   Menotti is the producer.   Five
paragraphs.

Mellen, Constance.   Musical Courier, CXLVIII (October,
1958), 33.
Review of the world premiere at the Brussels Exposition.   The reviewer considers the opera more
successful theatrically than musically.

"Menotti in New York. "   Opera News, XXIII (December 15,
1958), 14-15.
Review.   The opera is not successful.   Brief plot
summary.

"Menotti Revises 'Maria Golovine.' "   Opera, XXII (June,
1971), 529.
Review of the first performance of MARIA in a revised version at Marseilles in January, 1971.   The
performance is a success.   Menotti is the producer.
Plot summary.

"Menotti's Latest. "   Time, LXXII (September 1, 1958), 40.
Review of MARIA at Brussels.   The opera is a
"disappointment. "   Several lines of dialogue.   Photo
of Richard Cross as Donato and Franca Duval as
Maria.

"Milano. "   Rassegna Musicale, XXIX (March, 1959), 63-64.
Review of the La Scala production.

Mousset, Edouard.   "New Menotti Opera Receives Premiere

at Brussels. " Musical America, LXXVIII (October, 1958), 17.
Review of the world premiere. The NBC Opera Company performs the new work. It is called a success.

"Novo Menottijevo Delo. " Zvuk, XXIV-XXV (1959), 191-192.
Review. Three paragraphs.

"Opera in a Frenzy. " Newsweek, LII (September 1, 1958), 54.
Review. MARIA is warmly received at Brussels. Quotes from the composer on MARIA. He calls his characters "Proustian" and "more lyrical" than in his other works.

Peltz, Mary Ellis. "Menotti in Brussels. " Opera News, XXIX (September 29, 1959), 2-3.
Review of MARIA at the Brussel's Fair.

Rosen, George. "Fancy Brussels Premiere But Menotti's 'Maria Golovin' Not Grade-A Opera. " Variety, CCXI (August 27, 1958), 2+.
Review of the Brussels premiere. The opera's story is the most important part. There is little lyricism, only melodrama. There are no sustained arias and the recitatives carry the story. Cast members are all effective. Complete credits.

Sargeant, Winthrop. "Menotti Again. " New Yorker, XXXIV (November 15, 1958), 200-201.
Review at the Martin Beck Theatre. Sargeant thinks a bit of the music is eloquent. Menotti's devices, agony played against light music, do not work because the characters are ambiguous; thus any real force is lost. Sargeant likes the set number for the child's tutor. The production and cast are praised. In short, the weak characters heavily damage the work.

Schauensee, Max de. "Baltimore/Washington. " Opera, XVI (April, 1965), 279.
Review of the revised MARIA. The Opera Society of Washington performs it. One paragraph.

Severi, G. "'Maria Golovin' Ovvero Il Caso Menotti. " Musica d'Oggi, II (January, 1959), 14-16.

Review of the La Scala production which opens December 11. The cast and production team are given
in a box.

Smith, French Crawford. "Twin Capitals." Opera News,
XXIX (April 3, 1965), 31.
Short review of the premiere of the revised MARIA
given by the Washington Opera Society. Photo of
Donato (John Reardon) and Maria (Joan Marie
Moynagh).

Trimble, Leslie. Nation, CLXXXVII (November 22, 1958),
395-396.
Analysis of MARIA. Trimble considers the opera
an "aesthetic success." Menotti probably confused
the paying public by inviting only drama critics to
review MARIA. The story centers around the fates
of the usual Menottian trapped people. Trimble
charges that the philosophical ideas of the story are
never clarified, that the libretto is lacking. He
says the music is fresh and has vitality even though
some of the orchestral writing has a hastily composed sound. MARIA shows more than ever the
potential he has for being a great opera composer.
Brief plot summary.

MARTIN'S LIE

Barnes, Clive. "Mendacious Menotti." Music and Musi-
cians, XII (August, 1964), 22.
Review. Barnes says it is weak in musical interest.
Michael Wennink and Donald McIntyre are success-
ful as Martin and the Heretic. Plot summary.
Seven short paragraphs.

Cairns, David. "Bath Festival." Musical Times, CV (July
1964), 526.
Review of the world premiere of MARTIN'S LIE at
the Bath Festival in Bristol Cathedral. The music's
arrangement is praised. Plot summary and cast
listing.

_____. "Menotti's Lie." Spectator, CCXII (June 12,
1964), 794.
Article about MARTIN'S LIE at the Bath Festival
with reflections on THE TELEPHONE and THE

MEDIUM. Menotti's operatic formula appeals
greatly to those who cannot accept the usual operatic
conventions. Cairns charges that Menotti's music
does not communicate the drama. He feels MAR-
TIN'S LIE is mediocre. Only in THE TELEPHONE
is there no falseness in that the music and the
story complement each other. Cairns is critical
of THE MEDIUM for its cheap music and Menotti's
treatment of the subject matter. In MARTIN'S LIE
we are immediately aware of being played upon.
His message is confused. Seven paragraphs.

Guglielmi, Edoardo. "La 19 Sagra Musicale Umbra. " Musica
    d'Oggi, VII (n. 8, 1964), 232, 235-236.
    Review of the Italian premiere of LA BUGIA DI
    MARTIN at the church of San Angelo. Menotti has
    come from the political climate of THE CONSUL, a
    satire of civilization in THE LAST SAVAGE to the
    strong virtue in this story. Guglielmi is impressed
    by Menotti's control of dialectic, episodic construc-
    tion and psychological suggestions. But the religious
    material is sometimes "vague. " The music has
    echoes of Britten and Puccini. At its best this
    opera reminds one of AMAHL. Michael Wennink is
    intense as Martin. Other intelligent interpreters
    are Herbert Handt, Alberto Rinaldi, Giovanna
    Fioroni and Lorenzo Gaetani. Carlo Franci conducts
    well. Plot summary. Three paragraphs. Photo of
    the production.

Loveland, Kenneth. "Menottiho 'Martin Lhar' v Bristolu. "
    Hudebni Rozhledy, XVII (n. 14, 1964), 620.
    Review.

Maciejewski, B. M. "List z Londynu. " Ruch Muzyczny, XI
    (n. 19, 1964), 11.

"'Martin's Lie. ' " Opera, XV (Autumn, 1964), 34-35.
    Review of the premiere in Bristol Cathedral at the
    Bath Festival. Nothing about the opera is suited
    for a church except the final processional effect.
    This reviewer dislikes the morality, "the unearned
    redemption. " The performance is well done. Cast
    listing in a box and plot summary.

"Menotti in the Cathedral. " Newsweek, LXIII (June 15, 1964),
    93.

Review of the world premiere. The fifty minute
opera is the essence of simplicity with seven principals and a choir of boys. The story is of twelve-
year-old boy who needs a father and his hiding of a
pursued heretic. This critic finds the opera's
morality troubling. Three paragraphs. Photo of
Martin surrounded by other boys.

"A New Opera by Gian Carlo Menotti. " Show, IV (December,
      1964), 44-45.
            Libretto (G. Schirmer) and list of characters.
            Attractive drawings by Jean Hannon.

THE MEDIUM

"American Opera on Broadway. " Life, XXI (June, 1947),
      95-96, 98.
            Combination of photos and a page article, "'Medi-
            um's' Success Raises Hopes of Reviving a Moribund
            Art Form, " by Winthrop Sargeant. Sargeant thinks
            THE MEDIUM may prove that successful American
            operas can be produced. THE MEDIUM is an illus-
            tration that the work need not be a musical comedy.
            Past American operas have been largely flops. The
            Metropolitan Opera may not be the best spawning
            ground for American opera. Four photos of the
            Broadway production and one of Menotti.

Bauer, Leda. "Menotti Films 'The Medium'--One Man
      Show. " Theatre Arts, XXXV (October, 1951), 32-33+.
            Article about Menotti's direction of THE MEDIUM
            film. Bauer says Menotti has the rare privilege of
            realizing his own work on film exactly to his liking.
            The opera makes good theater. In horror literature
            the plot is an old type. Bauer calls it a Grand
            Guignol story. Menotti's biggest difficulties in film-
            ing are the story's static quality and brevity. Bauer
            thinks the added settings and outdoor scenes hurt
            the film. The theater setting evoked horror while
            Rome's sunshine does not. The macabre is lost in
            the film. Still the film is effective in its cast and
            music. Marie Powers, Anna Maria Alberghetti and Leo
            Coleman are excellent in their roles. THE MED-
            IUM needs color photography, not the used black
            and white. Photo of the hidden Toby looking at
            Mme. Flora and Monica.

Beyer, William. School and Society, LXVII (July 26, 1947),
    66.
    Sympathetic criticism. See also THE TELEPHONE.

_____, LXIX (January 29, 1949), 86.
    Brief review at the City Center Theater. See also
    THE TELEPHONE.

Brown, John Mason. "Seeing Things." Saturday Review,
    XXX (May 31, 1947), 22-24.
    Perceptive review of THE MEDIUM by the drama
    critic. This is one of the best early critiques of
    this opera and THE TELEPHONE as musical theater
    and drama. Virgil Thomson calls both "first-class"
    in the New York Herald Tribune. Olin Downes ac-
    claims both, also. Brown finds a good matching of
    music and drama in THE MEDIUM. In fact, neither
    would work by themselves. THE MEDIUM produc-
    tion is much the superior with an excellent set.
    Menotti's direction is effective for it. Marie
    Powers commands the stage so overwhelmingly as
    Mme. Flora that one forgets he is hearing opera
    and believes he is in the theater. Photo of Marie
    Powers. See also THE TELEPHONE.

"The Civilization of Musical Refuse Through 'The Medium' of
    Menotti." Musical Review, XIV (May, 1953), 141-143.
    Review of the opera and of the opera film. The
    reviewer is harshly critical of both. Scholarly dis-
    cussion of the keys used. The critic does not like
    his use of leitmotiv. The article closes with re-
    view excerpts of the filmed opera in Statesman, The
    Times, Daily Telegraph and Sunday Times.

"Contralto on Broadway." Time, XLIX (June 30, 1947), 69.
    Article about contralto Marie Powers who becomes
    widely identified with Madame Flora. Photo of
    Powers as Mme. Flora whipping Toby.

Cooper, Martin. Spectator, CLXXX (May 7, 1948), 554.
    Review of the opera at the Aldwych Theatre in Lon-
    don. Cooper applauds the singing and production.
    Marie Powers is Madame Flora, Evelyn Keller
    Monica. One paragraph.

Craig, Mary. "Menotti Opera Premiered." Musical Courier,
    CXXXV (March 1, 1947), 16.

THE MEDIUM performance is memorable. There
is an ovation for the company and composer. Photos
of Marie Powers and Menotti. See also THE TELE-
PHONE.

Deke, R. F.   "'The Medium.'" Film Music Notes, XI
     (September-October, 1951), 13-15.
     Careful analysis of THE MEDIUM musically and the
     way Menotti has his music work for the stage and
     screen. Musical examples from the score illustrate
     sonority, chromaticism, ground basses, prosody
     problems and so forth.

Demarquez, Suzanne. "Paris: Directorial Upheaval." Music
     Magazine/Musical Courier, CLXIV (May, 1962), 38.
     Review of the first performance at the Opera-
     Comique. The staging is not as Menotti specifies
     and is criticized. Photo of Menotti.

Ericson, Raymond. Musical America, LXXIX (May, 1959),
     89.
     Review at the New York City Opera. Claramae
     Turner sings Madame Flora.

Felton, James. "Temple Festival Gets a Roof Over Its
     Head." High Fidelity/Musical America, XXI (Novem-
     ber, 1971), MA 19, 22.
     Brief notice of a production at the Temple Univer-
     sity Festival. Muriel Greenspon excels in the title
     role. See also THE DEATH.

Goodman, John. "I Hear Wagner Singing." New Leader,
     LIII (August 17, 1970), 25-26.
     Review of Columbia's new recording. The opera is
     in the verismo style. Plot summary. Goodman
     finds it so sensational that he cannot take it seri-
     ously. The music is not adequate for the story's
     emotions.

Graf, Max. "Vienna Sees Double Bill of Menotti and Orff...."
     Musical America, LXXIII (April 15, 1953), 6.
     Review of an exciting Vienna State Opera production.
     Graf says some of the opera's great success must
     go to Adolf Rott's surrealistic staging. Photo of
     Rosette Anday (Mme. Flora) and her three clients.

Howe, Richard. "Hors d'Oeuvre, Meat and ... ?" Opera,

XIX (June, 1968), 486.
Compact review of the opera at the Opera-Comique
with Menotti as producer. Both are successful in
praised productions. See also THE TELEPHONE.

Jacobs, Arthur. "Ambler, Pennsylvania. " Musical Times,
CXII (September, 1971), 889.
Tiny review of THE MEDIUM at the Temple Uni-
versity Music Festival and Institute. Muriel Green-
spon is a strong Madame Flora. See also THE
DEATH.

Kolodin, Irving. "Murder and Mirth. " Saturday Review of
Literature, XXXI (January 31, 1948), 44.
Review of the Columbia recording of THE MEDIUM
paired with THE TELEPHONE. Kolodin concludes
that the recorded music is even better than in the
theater. See also THE TELEPHONE.

Krutch, Joseph Wood. Nation, CLXIV (May 24, 1947), 637-
638.
Review of the melodrama in a production at the
Ethel Barrymore Theatre. See also THE TELE-
PHONE.

Lardner, John. "Low Crimes and Singing Plays. " New
Yorker, XXIII (May 10, 1947), 50, 52.
Review at the Ethel Barrymore Theatre. See also
THE TELEPHONE.

Mari, Pierrette. "Creation D'Amelia Va au Bal' au Cours
d'un Gala Menotti a Metz. " Journal Musical Francais,
CLXVIII (April, 1968), 40-41.
Review of a production at Metz. Menotti shows
much knowledge of orchestration. The music must
reach for the pathetic. The cast at its best achieves
the richness of feeling necessary to the roles.
Lucienne Delvaux has a triumph with a Mme. Flora
of "perfect articulation. " Other singers are Jacqueline Danjou (Monica), Odette Remy and Jacques
Herbillon (the Gobineaus) and Janine Capderou (Mrs.
Nolan). Abel Rilliard's directing touches Mari in
the children's duet. Marcel Bloys is an excellent
mime as Toby. Rilliard's set catches all details.
Michel Plasson is the excellent conductor of the
Metz orchestra. See also AMELIA.

"'Le Medium.'" Opera de Paris, (n. 21, 1962), 22.
Photos: Monique de Pondeau (Monica), Marc Du-
Champ (Toby) and Denise Scharley (Mme. Flora).

"'The Medium' on Film." New York Times Magazine, C
(April 8, 1951), 60-61.
Article about the film version. Menotti composes
twenty minutes of new music. The leads are Marie
Powers, Anna Maria Alberghetti and Leo Coleman.
Four photos from the film: Madame Flora (Marie
Powers imagining a hand on her throat), Monica
(Anna Maria Alberghetti) and Toby (Leo Coleman)
play, Monica (her lighted face) and Mme. Flora
flogs Toby.

Menotti, Gian-Carlo. "'The Medium' in Four Mediums."
Saturday Review, XXXI (February 28, 1948), 43-44.
Menotti discusses the "artistic dilemma" of stage-
works being recorded. The problems of adapting
scripts for various degrees of "improving" are considered. He talks about the possibilities of filming
the opera. Valuable for his view of THE MEDIUM.

"Menotti and the Movie 'Medium.'" Saturday Review, XXXIV
(September 8, 1951), 36.
Review of THE MEDIUM film. The opera comes
close to being what opera should be on film. Menotti
dominates with his sense of sound drama.

"Opera in Embryo." Newsweek, XXIX (March 3, 1947), 76.
Short review at the Heckscher Playhouse in New
York. It is a revised production. Photo of Menotti.
See also THE TELEPHONE.

Phelan, Kappo. Commonweal, XLV (March 7, 1947), 518-
519.
Review. Carefully considered comments. See also
THE TELEPHONE.

Rigault, Jean de. "A Menotti Rien D'Impossible." La Revue
Musicale, CCXI (March, 1952), 33-35.
Review of the film premiere in Paris. After Abel
Gance's failure with the Louise film, Menotti shows
it is possible to join "lyrical drama" with the
camera. This accomplishment is due to Menotti's
personal conception and realization. Changes include new scenes, transitions and over twenty

minutes of new music. Most of the music is not
filler material except for one or two places, e. g.,
the children playing in front of their grieved
parents. His music makes a counterpoint between
Flora's anguish and the idyllic world of Monica with
Toby. The writer points to one moment when these
two worlds meet in the "language of the soul. " In
contrast to the stage's one room setting, the film
has outdoor scenes which Rigault thinks are justified
for the "progression of the fixed idea" in the story.
Menotti gives more time also to the Toby-Monica
relationship. Menotti has not made a "recipe" for
future opera films, but he illustrates the results
when the composer is inspired to recast an original
musical form. With the aid of the Italian film
technicians, this is a "masterpiece" in the cinema
of lyric works. He praises Marie Powers, Anna
Maria Alberghetti, Leo Coleman and conductor
Thomas Schippers. Seven large paragraphs.

Sabin, Robert. "Film Version of 'The Medium' Directed by
Menotti in Rome. " Musical America, LXXI (April 15,
1951), 21.
Review of the film production. Menotti has added
new scenes to the film. Sabin comments on all
roles and the milieu established.

Sargeant, Winthrop. New Yorker, XXXIX (May 18, 1963), 96.
Review at the New York City Opera. Lili Chookasian is strong as Mme. Flora. See also AMELIA.

Shawe-Taylor, Desmond. "Something New. " New Statesman,
XXXV (May 8, 1948), 372.
Review at the Aldwych Theater in London. Menotti's
invention is slighter than that of Albert Herring.
The opera has real irony. Marie Powers is strik-
ing as the Medium. See also THE TELEPHONE.

Smith, Cecil. "Menotti Double Bill Returns in Arena-Style
Production. " Musical America, LXX (August, 1950),
17.
Review of THE MEDIUM at the Arena, formerly a
dining room of the Hotel Edison. Smith argues that
the theater in the round arrangement damages the
illusion of THE MEDIUM and is not effective as a
proscenium arch from a distance. The final paragraph is a discussion of Zelma George's highly

individual interpretation of Mme. Flora. With photo
of the composer, George and Patricia Neway.

_____. New Republic, CXVI (March 10, 1947), 40-41.
Short review. See also THE TELEPHONE.

"The Talk of the Town. " New Yorker, XXIII (June 7, 1947),
23-24.
Article with earlier biographical material. There
is an explanation of how the idea for THE MEDIUM
originates in Austria and humorous material on
Marie Power's problem of killing Toby in the production.

"Three Operas From Group 8, the March St. Pancras Festi-
val. " Music and Musicians, IX (May, 1961), 15.
Photos: Monica Sinclair (Mme. Flora) with playing
cards; Audrey Deakin (Monica) with Tony Calvin
(Toby); and Mme. Flora with her clients played by
Rita McKerrow, George MacPherson and Peggy
Castle.

"Unblessed by the Met. " Time, XLVII (May 20, 1946), 56.
Article primarily about THE MEDIUM, the world
premiere. The mute is hailed for his portrayal.
Photo of Menotti.

"Uptown. " New Yorker, XXII (May 18, 1946), 96-97.
Review of the world premiere at Columbia University. The performance is termed a success.

"Ventures in Lyric Theatre. " Theatre Arts, XXXI (May,
1947), 60-61.
Review of a double bill at the Heckscher Theatre.
The writer feels THE MEDIUM shows more care in
composing than the lighter work. See also THE
TELEPHONE.

Weaver, William. "Falla/Menotti Bill. " High Fidelity/
Musical America, XIX (October, 1969), MA 30-31.
Review of THE MEDIUM at Spoleto. The production
and performance is a grand success.

_____. "Menotti and Rossini at Spoleto. " Opera, XX
(Autumn, 1969), 112-113.
Review of the Spoleto production sung in Italian.
Muriel Greenspon is an exceptional Mme. Flora.

Pier Luigi Samaritani's sets and costumes contribute
to its success. Two paragraphs. Photo of Greenspon, Joanna Bruno (Monica) and Frank Phelan
(Toby).

Whitebait, William. "'The Medium' at the Academy. " New
    Statesman and Nation, XLV (March 28, 1953), 368.
    Review of the film version. Whitebait calls the
    film exciting, the "cinema's first opera. " Menotti
    shows unusual insights in making his opera effective
    on film. Five paragraphs.

Wyatt, Euphemia Van Rensselaer. Catholic World, CLXV
    (June, 1947), 265-266.
    Review. Consideration of the opera as opera or
    drama. See also THE TELEPHONE.

_____. Catholic World, CLXXI (September, 1950), 469.
    Review of a performance at the Arena. The staging
    changes are discussed. Zelma George is lauded for
    her Mme. Flora. Three paragraphs. See also
    THE TELEPHONE.

THE MOST IMPORTANT MAN

Bender, William. "Living Children. " Time, XCVII (March
    22, 1971), 59.
    · Review article about the world premiere at the New
    York City Opera. The opening is postponed six
    days so Menotti can finish his composition. He has
    a block in writing as evidenced by his struggles to
    complete AMAHL. In this opera his music is tradi-
    tional early 20th century. Bender believes the opera
    breaks no new paths for him, but its orchestration
    and certain arias could make it popular with Menotti
    fans. Menotti is not worried about his old-fashioned
    image among contemporary composers. He rejects
    atonality but perhaps fails to see this form's free-
    dom for modern expression. His is an important
    historic role in today's opera. Seven paragraphs.
    Photo of Joanna Bruno (Cora) and Eugene Holmes
    (Toime).

Freeman, John W. Opera News, XXXV (April 17, 1971), 29.
    Review of the world premiere March 7 at the New
    York City Opera. The imaginative new work is not

as entertaining as THE LAST SAVAGE, but the
music has freshness and creativity.   There is
praise for all.   Photo of Cora (Joanna Bruno) and
Toime (Eugene Holmes).

Kolodin, Irving.   Saturday Review, LIV (March 27, 1971), 16.
   Review at the New York City Opera.   The assess-
   ment is that the opera is easily forgettable.
   Menotti's central problem of racial prejudice is not
   sufficient for real impulse musically.   The melody
   is more Tosca than the Veldt.   Kolodin has praise
   for many valiant efforts in an "unhappy problem. "
   Brief plot summary.

Movshon, George.   "'The Most Important Man. '"   High
   Fidelity/Musical America, XXI (June, 1971), MA 16.
   Review.   Movshon notes that critics Alan Rich and
   Winthrop Sargeant are pleased with this new work.
   Movshon finds it flat and unreal; the libretto is thin.
   The musical score is second rate.   Beverly Wolff
   and Eugene Holmes are praised in the cast.   Four
   paragraphs.   Photo of Eugene Holmes (Toime) and
   Joanna Bruno (Cora) in the New York City Opera
   production.

Opera, XXII (June, 1971), 507.
   Review of the March 21 matinee in New York.   It is
   considered a failure in terms other than its "message. "

"Opera Review. "   Variety, CCLXII (March 17, 1971), 74.
   Review that is largely negative.   Eugene Holmes,
   Joanna Bruno and Beverly Wolff all are effective,
   but the opera is uninteresting.   Haste and question-
   able judgment are apparent in the production.   The
   plot is too predictable.   The score is derived from
   earlier Menotti.   Weaknesses in the story damage
   the opera.   For example, the black scientist has
   lines that are totally unsuited for a modern scientist
   and there is no dramatic motivation for Dr. Arnek,
   the master.   Menotti's handling of racial conflict is
   caricature.   The critic says a scene of white poli-
   ticians has the most interest.   Cast and production
   credits.

Saal, Hubert.   "The Preacher. "   Newsweek, LXXVII (March
   29, 1971), 92-93.

Review.   Saal claims that the production including
the performances is the best thing about THE MOST
IMPORTANT MAN.   In the first half Menotti is
more successful.   But finally he deals more with
issues than with people.   Photo of Eugene Holmes
(Toime) and Joanna Bruno (Cora).

Sargeant, Winthrop.   "Sci-Fi in the Veldt. "   New Yorker,
XLVII (March 20, 1971), 132.
Review of the world premiere at the New York City
Opera.   Sargeant finds the new opera one of
Menotti's most impressive.   Sargeant praises the
characters, cast and some of the music.   As a
whole he calls it "highly effective. "   Good plot sum-
mary.

Trebor, Emil.   Music Journal, XXIX (May, 1971), 69-70.
Review.   It is "moderately successful. "   The reviewer recommends rewriting of the later acts to
bring them to the level of the first act.   Two paragraphs.

Weinstock, Herbert.   "New York. "   Opera, XXII (June, 1971),
507-508.
Review of the March 21 matinee at the New York
City Opera.   Weinstock says the score is banal,
the melodies not very expressive.   Eugene Holmes
makes a striking Toime.   The opera may be a
"disaster. "   One paragraph.   Photo of Beverly
Wolff (Leona Arnek), Joanna Bruno (Cora Arnek)
and Eugene Holmes (Toime).

THE OLD MAID AND THE THIEF

"Actor's Ensemble. "   Counterpoint, XVIII (February, 1953),
32-33.
Review at the Playhouse in San Francisco.   The
reviewer is enthusiastic about the opera as theatre
and music.   One sizable paragraph.

"C'est La Guerre. "   The Musician, XLIX (April, 1944), 69.
THE OLD MAID is taken to army camps and hos-
pitals by the Juilliard School during World War II.
Plot summary, listing of Juilliard students and their
roles.

Diamond, David. "Over the Air." Modern Music, XVI (May-
    June, 1939), 271-272.
        Review. Diamond is enthusiastic about the work as
        opera buffa, less about the composing style. He
        says Menotti is a sincere, unpretentious composer.

Eaton, Quaintance. "Menotti's 'Amahl and the Night Visitors'
    Second Novelty of the Spring Season." Musical
    America, LXXII (April 15, 1952), 5+.
        Review of one paragraph at the City Center. See
        also AMAHL.

McDonald, Dennis. "'Amahl' Hit." Billboard, LXIV (April
    19, 1952), 48.
        Review. Mary Kreste sings in the production. See
        also AMAHL.

Marx, Henry. "Failure and Success at the City Center."
    Music News, XLV (May, 1952), 4.
        Review at the City Center. It should always amuse.
        See also AMAHL.

"Menotti Bis." Slovenska Hudba, XI (n. 10, 1967), 453-454.
        Review. Four paragraphs. Photo of Bob, Laetitia
        and Miss Todd. $23255 \rvert$

"Menotti-Oper in der Wiener Volksoper." Oesterreichische
    Musikzeitschrift, XVI (April, 1961), 179.
        Review of THE OLD MAID at the Vienna Volksoper.
        The set shows an entire house. Olive Moorefield
        is very charming as the servant. Heinz Holecek is
        less effective as the wanderer. Hans Jaray con-
        ducts well. The large set has caused the director
        to introduce actions that are sometimes unnatural.
        There is the problem of balancing a weak story with
        an empty stage. Over half a page.

"Menotti Radio Opera is Premiered." Musical Courier,
    CXIX (May 1, 1939), 4.
        Review of the premiere on NBC Radio April 22.
        The music and libretto are praised. Plot summary
        and cast listing.

"Menotti's 'Amahl' Staged at New York City Center." Musical
    Courier, CXLV (May 1, 1952), 11.
        One sentence notice. See also AMAHL.

"Opera Can Be Fun. " Time, LI (April 19, 1948), 50.
        Review of THE OLD MAID on a double bill. Photo
        of Marie Powers and Virginia MacWatters in THE
        OLD MAID. See also AMELIA.

"Radio Opera. " Time, XXXII (May 1, 1939), 56-57.
        Review of the premiere radio performance. It
        satirizes women as did AMELIA. The studio audi-
        ence feels Menotti has a success. Plot summary.
        Photo of Menotti.

"Ricecare and Toccata on a Theme from 'The Old Maid and
        the Thief. ' " Musical Courier, CL (September, 1954),
        43.
        Description of the music from a theme from THE
        OLD MAID published by G. Ricordi.

Smith, Cecil. "Music: Operatic Gagster. " New Republic,
        CXVIII (April 26, 1948), 36-37.
        Review of a performance at the New York City
        Center. Smith says THE OLD MAID is between
        opera and comedy. It is a less careful work than
        AMELIA. See also AMELIA.

Sternfeld, Frederick W. "Ricecare and Toccata on a Theme
        from 'The Old Maid and the Thief' for Piano. " Music
        Library Association Notes, XII (March, 1955), 329.
        Analytic article. Sternfeld thinks this "puzzling"
        piece is better as an operatic theme than for solo
        piano. He criticizes the ricercare for its absence
        of polyphony. One paragraph.

Theatre Arts, XXIX (July, 1945), 29.
        Photo of a production at Western Reserve Univer-
        sity in Cleveland.

Theatre Arts, XXX (July, 1946), 382.
        Photo of a production at the University of Michigan.
        All four characters are shown.

Watts, Douglas. "Large and Small. " New Yorker, XXVIII
        (April 19, 1952), 91.
        Review of THE OLD MAID at the City Center.
        Watts says it is given routinely. See also AMELIA.

THE SAINT OF BLEECKER STREET

Blitzstein, Marc. "'The Saint of Bleecker Street.'" Music
  Library Association Notes, XIII (June, 1956), 521-523.
    Blitzstein, a composer, notes the chilly reception
    THE SAINT receives in Europe. He says Menotti's
    greatest stumbling block is his choice of theme or
    his failure to make the theme of the church versus
    skepticism work. Menotti succeeds in scenes with
    the church motif, but he has not developed Michele,
    the representative of skepticism. Possibly it is
    more of an "Italian" opera. Blitzstein analyzes
    various reactions to the opera.

Bremini, Ireneo. Opera, XXI (February, 1970), 123.
    Review of a successful SAINT at Trieste. One
    paragraph.

Clurman, Harold. Nation, CLXXX (January 22, 1955), 83.
    Review. Clurman says if he is to have sympathy,
    he must look at the "symbolic undertones." He
    gives his interpretation of the plot. Clurman can-
    not take the action literally. Five paragraphs.

"Concert Records." New Yorker, XXXI (June 4, 1955), 111-
  112.
    Review of the RCA Victor recording. The reviewer
    discusses the credibility of the characters, the end-
    ing, "structural flaws" and what he considers to be
    the composer's natural musical idiom.

Cowles, Chandler. "A Broadway Bailiwick for Opera."
  Theatre Arts, XXXIX (January, 1955), 72-73+.
    A consideration of the possibilities for opera on
    Broadway as popular entertainment. THE SAINT is
    the fourth Menotti opera Cowles has helped to pro-
    duce on Broadway. He points out that a producer
    for Menotti is more limited since the composer is
    his own stage director. In THE SAINT the conflict
    is a contemporary one built around man's relation
    to God and to the world. The production for this
    work is unconventional, but so are the libretto and
    the music. Cowles believes Menotti's successes on
    Broadway should encourage other opera composers.

Dunlop, Lionel. "Kentish Opera Group Season." Opera,
  XIII (September, 1962), 634-635.

Review. Dunlop is revolted by the work, its religious material. The singing cast is generally
good as is the production. Brief plot summary.
Five paragraphs.

Fiechtner, Helmut A. "'Die Heilige aus der Bleecker Street'
zum Erstenmal auf Deutsch." Melos, XXII (November, 1955), 333.
Review. Menotti uses several idioms--Puccini,
Gregorian liturgical, blues. Camilla Williams is
an excellent Annina. Four paragraphs.

_____. "'Die Heilige von der Bleecker Street.'" Musica
(Kassel), IX (November, 1955), 558-559.
Review of a Vienna Volksoper production. Excerpted quote from Menotti in Perspektiven on bash-
ful modern dramatists. Menotti uses the ideas of
superstition, materialism, Americanism, incest,
jealousy for strong theater. His music is associated with Puccini and Mussorgsky. The critic notes
his skill using dissimilar musical forms--Gregorian
music, Neopolitan wedding songs, blues and Gershwin. Herbert Graf is the stage director. Camilla
Williams is a touching, believable Annina. Other
cast members are listed. Heinrich Hollreiser conducts. Plot summary.

Geitel, Klaus. "Wagnis Mit Wagner." Opern Welt, IX
(September, 1968), 22-23.
Review of a Spoleto production. It is a return to
Puccini.

Golea, Antoine. "Naturgetreues Operntheater in Spoleto."
Neue Zeitschrift fur Musik (September, 1968), 382-384.

Goth, Gisella Selden. Musical Courier, CLI (June, 1955), 25.
Short review of its first European performance at
La Scala. The Italian audience responds with enthusiasm. The composer as usual is the stage
director.

Graf, Max. "Vienna Hears New York Group and Latest
Menotti Opera." Musical America, LXXV (October,
1955), 34.
Review of a performance in the Volksoper sung in
German for the first time. Graf thinks the opera
is theatrically exciting.

Hayes, Richard. Commonweal, LXI (February 4, 1955), 476-
477.
Review. THE SAINT adds up to a real experience
although one may be disturbed by it. Hayes feels
Menotti has neglected "truth" and aesthetics in his
employment of "effect. " We overlook the moral
truths and are attracted by the externalness of THE
CONSUL and THE SAINT. The protagonists cannot
really do battle in this opera because Michele is
too weak a character. The music is eclectic; the
true triumph is the music of the final scene, Annina's consecration. Hayes comments on individual
performances. Five large paragraphs.

Holde, Arthur. "Die Jungste Menotti-Oper am New Yorker
Broadway. " Musikleben, VIII (February, 1955), 59.
Review. Holde is uncertain whether THE SAINT
will enjoy a long run similar to THE CONSUL's.
The first public hearing is a success. In contrast
to THE CONSUL, the orchestra sounds more "vivid"
and the melodies are of a higher order. Tosca's
influence is felt but Menotti is still very original.
The composer's talent for directing is cited in the
dramatic scenes of Annina's stigmata and the interruption of the wedding festivities by the murder of
Desideria. Unlike the content of THE CONSUL,
society is not accused and the scenes do not build
up to a logical, inevitable catastrophe. Such suspense can make one sympathetic to textual weaknesses. Holde believes more suspense could have
been achieved in the subway scene if irrelevent details had been omitted. The singers are excellent
in voice and acting. The audience reacts with enthusiasm. Six paragraphs.

Kessler, Hansi. " 'Tristan' und Menotti. " Musica, XXII
(November-December, 1968), 468.
Review of the Spoleto production. Two paragraphs.

Kirstein, Lincoln. "The Future of American Opera. "
Atlantic Monthly, CLXXXIX (March, 1957), 55.
Commentary on what THE SAINT is to Kirstein. He
sees a definite debt to Mussorgsky in this work.

_____. "Menotti: The Giants in Bleecker Street. "
Center, I (December, 1954), 3-8.
Excellent analysis. This new work combines

Menotti's past in vocal writing with his talents as a
theatrical producer. THE SAINT is on a grand
scale, large scale characters, large choruses and
meaty solo and duet pieces. Bleecker Street is one
of the world's oldest Italian colonies. The tragedy
is built from Mediterranean and Atlantic cultures.
Part of Michele's aria, "Look at Yourselves," is
quoted. Michele struggles to assimilate himself
into America. Annina is based on the Bavarian
Therese Neumann who had deep palm wounds which
she believed to be stigmata. Since Menotti is
assuming a strong Catholic atmosphere he creates
a basis for the faith versus reason conflict. THE
SAINT points up the crisis modernist painters face
in constantly seeking to innovate and to be always
extremely individual. Menotti has rejected the usual
modernism of seeking to disturb the audience with a
strong musical language. There is a "three-di-
mensional visual projection" in Menotti. Visually
THE SAINT has a real identification with George
Tooker, a young Brooklyn painter whose Subway
hangs in the Whitney Museum of American Art.
Good discussion of the relationship between Tooker
and Menotti in THE SAINT. The subway is the
setting in the last act. THE SAINT is the model of
an expert libretto recalling the work of Scribe,
Sardou and Belasco, theatre of grandeur. Its story
is a parable with familiar elements reaching the
status of archetypes. George Tooker's painting,
Festa, suggests the second act setting of the San
Gennaro festival. Other illustrations are two paint-
ings, Fortune Teller (1952) and Juke Box (1952).

Koegler, Horst. Musical Courier, CLII (December 1, 1955),
    31.
    Review of the German premiere at the Stadtische
    Oper in Berlin. Berlin critics do not take to the
    work. Koegler praises the Berlin production and
    the four principals. Three paragraphs.

Kolodin, Irving. "Menotti's 'The Saint of Bleecker Street.'"
    Saturday Review, XXXVIII (January 28, 1955), 29.
    Good review. Kolodin's understanding of how
    Menotti achieves theatrical success and serves
    theatrical ends is striking. As so many do, Kolo-
    din connects Menotti with the Grand Guignol school
    while noting his development as a composer.

Levinger, Henry W. Musical Courier, CLI (January 15,
     1955), 13-14.
          Review of THE SAINT that is very favorable. Plot
          summary.

Mahlke, E. and Schweizer, G. "'Die Heilige von der
     Bleecker Street.'" Musica, X (January, 1956), 84-86.
          Review of productions in Berlin and Wiesbaden.
          Mahlke feels the subject is "disgusting." There is
          no excuse for the manner in which Menotti mixes
          Catholic ritual, sex, violence and other elements.
          An imaginative director can do much with Annina's
          visions. Thomas Schippers conducts. The cast is
          a strong one with Elfride Triotschel singing Annina,
          Mimi Aarden the prostitute and Sandor Konya the
          brother. Mahlke criticizes the audience for its
          strong applause. Schweizer reviews the Wiesbaden
          premiere. THE SAINT causes one to react either
          pro or con as Menotti believes musical theater
          should. Lead roles are sung by Hannelore Backrass
          (Annina), Susanne Muser (Desideria) and Martin
          Kremer (Michele). The audience is enthusiastic.
          Plot synopsis in the Schweizer review. Six large
          paragraphs.

Malipiero, Riccardo. Opera, VI (July, 1955), 451-452.
          Review. THE SAINT is a hit with the public but
          not with critics in its La Scala premiere May 8.
          Malipiero charges it is an "ugly score" without
          originality. Photo of the second act at La Scala
          with Gloria Lane (Desideria), Gabriella Ruggiero
          (Annina) and David Poleri (Michele).

Mannes, Marya. "Broadway Speculations." Reporter, XII
     (April 7, 1955), 40.
          Article about the relative lack of success for THE
          SAINT on Broadway. Mannes asks why the opera
          is having box office troubles after such good re-
          views. The larger theater audience has withdrawn
          its support. Mannes thinks the human motivation of
          the opera is hazy and that because of the opera's
          Catholic aura, many non-Catholics are offended.
          Ordinarily there is great theater support from Jews
          in New York. For THE SAINT even the Catholic
          audience has stayed away.

"Menotti's New ' Tristan.'" High Fidelity/Musical America,

XVIII (September, 1968), MA 30.
Brief mention of THE SAINT at the Spoleto festival.
Gloria Lane sings Desideria.

"Opera Review. " Down Beat, VIII (February 9, 1955), 8.
Review of THE SAINT at the Broadway Theatre.
The run is a "hit. " Four paragraphs. Photo of
David Poleri (Michele) and Gloria Lane (Desideria).

Osborne, C. L. "Spring Comes to City Center. " High
Fidelity/Musical America, XV (June, 1965), 116-117+.
Review of the opera at the City Center. Osborne
admits that Menotti clearly knows how to make
theater in opera even if he sometimes overreaches
himself in ideas and characters. Menotti makes
this reviewer care about the three leading characters.

"People Are Talking About.... " Vogue, CXXV (February,
1955), 144-145.
One paragraph, mostly on THE SAINT. The public
is excited about the work, pro or con. Full page
drawing of Menotti.

Reich, Willi. "Menotti's 'Heilige der Bleecker Street.' "
Melos, XXIII (March, 1956), 85.
Review of a production in Basel. THE SAINT was
not well received at La Scala by the critics or in
Wien, but it is successful in Basel. Two para-
graphs.

Sabin, Robert. "Menotti's Latest Opera Given Broadway Premiere. " Musical America, LXXV (January 15, 1955),
324.
Excellent review of THE SAINT with a clear plot
summary. Two paragraphs. Two photos.

"Saint, But No Sinner. " International Musician, LIII (February, 1955), 11.
Review. The reviewer sees similarities in Parsifal
and this work. But unlike Parsifal's strengths he
notes serious weaknesses in Menotti's plot and his
text.

"'The Saint of Bleecker Street.' " Newsweek, XLV (January
10, 1955), 62.
Review. The conclusion is that the plot is weak,

but Menotti's music makes the opera one worth ex-
periencing.

"'The Saint of Bleecker Street.'" Opera, VII (November,
1956), 703-704.
Review of a television production on BBC. The reviewer discusses the techniques employed by Rudolf
Cartier such as the problems of closeups while
singing. Puccini's influence is very noticeable in
music that is memorable. The principals are
praised.

"'The Saint of Bleecker Street.'" Opera News, XIX (January 24, 1955), 15.
Short review of the Broadway Theatre production
with brief excerpts from reviews by Olin Downes,
Walter Kerr and Jay Harrison. Four photos.

"'The Saint of Bleecker Street.'" Variety, CLXXXVII (December 29, 1954), 48.
Review of the Broadway Theatre production. The
opera is called excellent entertainment. The roles
are well sung. The stage management is very
effective, but the message is uncertain. Gloria
Lane as Desideria stops the show. Menotti is skillful in handling religion. Max Reinhardt's "The
Miracle" is compared to the opera. Annina's vows
make for "high theatre." Certain sections suggest
good possibilities for the screen. Complete cast
and production credits.

"Saint Song." Vogue, CXXIV (December, 1954), 114-115.
Reproduction of the G. Schirmer publication of
Annina's aria, "But once in the deep of night
Michael the archangel came to me." First twenty-
seven bars through the phrase, "You will sing the
praise of Christ our Lord."

Sargeant, Winthrop. "Menotti's New Opera." New Yorker,
XXX (January 8, 1955), 74-76.
Review of the Broadway production. Although
Sargeant says it is effective theater, he thinks some
of Menotti's problems with the characters' behavior
takes away force. THE SAINT illustrates how weak
piety can be as an operatic theme. Annina is too
good to be convincing. As a result Desideria with
her real weaknesses is the strongest character.

Gloria Lane is a great success as Desideria.

Sargeant, Winthrop. New Yorker, XLI (March 27, 1965), 172.
Review of a New York City Opera revival. One
substantial paragraph.

Seelmann-Eggebert, Ulrich. "New Italy in Vecchia Italia."
Musikleben, VIII (September, 1955), 325.
Review. There are twenty-five curtain calls after
the final act. Some of the applause ought to go to
Puccini and Massenet for their influence. This is
Menotti at his most mature. The score has rich
musical content with effective ensembles and some
Gershwin rhythms. Menotti successfully integrates
the liturgical music. He unites the Neopolitan
wedding songs, American blues and sounds like the
subway thunder and the police siren in a manner
reminiscent of Italian verismo. Some of the success at La Scala may be attributed to Italian patriotism
associated with the "New Italy" of New York City. The
critic says this like THE MEDIUM is ripe for screen
treatment since visual effects are so prominent. Also,
the writer thinks Michele comes across like a Marlon
Brando. Gabrielle Ruggiero is praised as Annina.
Whether the work will appeal to German audiences is
uncertain. Four large paragraphs.

"Successful 'Saint.'" Time, LXV (January 10, 1955), 42.
Review. Plot summary. Sections of the musical
score are included. Photo of Virginia Copeland as
the Saint.

Wyatt, Euphemia Van Rensselaer. Catholic World, CLXXX
(February, 1955), 385.
Review of the Broadway production. Wyatt thinks
this is Menotti's finest score and praises the work.
Plot summary.

Zoff, O. "'Die Heilige Aus der Bleecker Street' in New York
Uraufgefuhrt." Melos, XXII (February, 1955), 57-58.
Review. THE SAINT is strongly Italian verismo.
The opposing sides are the traditional Catholicism
and a newer anti-religion. This is apparently not
a melodrama. Compared to the liturgical rapture
of Annina, the conflict is not made important. Puccini's influence is obvious. Several episodes honor
the discriminating hearer.

Zolotow, Maurice. Theatre Arts, XXXIX (March, 1955), 17,
 22-23.
  Analysis. Good synopsis of the story. Zolotow
  expects the new opera to be the most significant
  production of the season. Menotti has a prodigious
  ambition. There is great homogeneity since he has
  stamped the work with his personal creativity.
  Zolotow asserts that Menotti is unsure of his theme,
  that he himself is torn between Roman Catholicism
  and disbelief. His confusion is most evident in the
  brother-sister relationship. To Zolotow incest is
  the opera's real conflict but is ambiguous. What
  Menotti needs is a great composer of melody such
  as Verdi for his superb librettos. Zolotow compares him to Boito, Verdi's librettist for Otello.

THE TELEPHONE

Beyer, William. School and Society, LXVII (July 26, 1947),
 66-67.
  Brief review. See also THE MEDIUM.

_____. School and Society, LXIX (January 29, 1949), 86.
  Brief review at the City Center. Beyer is pleased
  by a new cast, Maria D'Attili and Paul King and the
  "melodic" score.

Brown, John Mason. "Seeing Things." Saturday Review of
 Literature, XXX (May 31, 1947), 22-24.
  Perceptive review. Brown does not find THE
  TELEPHONE "amusing" as Olin Downes does. He
  thinks it is too trifling for thirty minutes. He is
  critical of Menotti's direction and the "unengaging"
  acting of the two principals. Some of the soprano's
  singing into the phone is ridiculous to him. See
  also THE MEDIUM.

Chiesa, Mary T. "New Operas in an Ancient Theater."
 Musical Courier, CXXXVIII (November 15, 1948), 5.
  Review of one paragraph at the 11th International
  Music Festival in Venice.

Cooper, Martin. Spectator, CLXXX (May 7, 1948), 554.
  Brief review of THE TELEPHONE at the Aldwych
  Theatre in London. To Cooper the opera is a
  "sketch." Menotti reminds him of Rossini, Poulenc

and other French composers of the 1920's without
the same type of parody. The music has a cant-
abile quality. Plot summary.

Craig, Mary. "Menotti Opera Premiered. " Musical Courier,
    CXXXV (March 1, 1947), 16.
        Review. THE TELEPHONE at the Heckscher
        Theatre. It has much gaiety about it. Menotti's
        orchestration shows skill. Both Marilyn Cotlow and
        Paul Kwartin are successful as Lucy and Ben. Plot
        in a nutshell. Photo of Cotlow. See also THE
        MEDIUM.

Heller, E. "Telephongespraeche in der Wiener Kammeroper."
    Oesterreichische Musikzeitschrift, XXVI (February,
    1971), 97-98.

Howe, Richard. "Hors d'Oeuvre, Meat and... ?" Opera,
    XIX (June, 1968), 486.
        Compact review at the Opera-Comique with Menotti
        as producer. It is successful. See also THE
        MEDIUM.

Kolodin, Irving. "Murder and Mirth. " Saturday Review,
    XXXI (January 31, 1948), 44.
        Review of the Columbia recording. It is exactly
        correct in its length. Marilyn Cotlow has excellent
        diction and sings the role superbly. One paragraph.
        Photo of Menotti. See also THE MEDIUM.

Krutch, Joseph Wood. Nation, CLXIV (May 24, 1947), 637-
    638.
        Review of a performance at the Ethel Barrymore
        Theatre. Krutch finds THE TELEPHONE of interest
        as a music drama. It is merely a "revue sketch. "

Lardner, John. "Low Crimes and Singing Plays. " New
    Yorker, XXIII (May 10, 1947), 50, 52.
        Short review of the production at the Ethel Barry-
        more Theatre. It is sometimes "pretentious. "
        Menotti may have harmed the impact of the follow-
        ing MEDIUM because one looks for the same "thin"
        talk in it after the one-act comedy. Marilyn Cotlow
        and Frank Rogier are winning performers. See
        also THE MEDIUM.

"Opera in Embryo. " Newsweek, XXXIX (March 3, 1947), 76.

Article about the world premiere at the Heckscher
Playhouse. Brief synopsis. One paragraph. Photo
of Menotti. See also THE MEDIUM.

"Opera in Small Packages. " Time, XLIX (March 3, 1947),
65.
Short article on the world premiere. The writer
considers it a slight work. It requires only a thir-
teen-piece orchestra. Menotti points out THE
TELEPHONE is not "grand enough" for Italy. Plot
in a nutshell. Photo of Menotti with the Lucy and
Ben.

Phelan, Kappo. Commonweal, XLV (March 7, 1947), 518.
Short review. Phelan thinks THE TELEPHONE is
entertaining but the acting "stilted" and Horace
Armistead's setting unsatisfactory. See also THE
MEDIUM.

Razboynikov, S. "Tri Ednoaktni Operi na Sofiyska Stsena. "
Bulgarska Muzika, XIX (n. 4, 1968), 50-53.
Review. Photo of the principals.

Shawe-Taylor, Desmond. "Something New. " New Statesman,
XXXV (May 8, 1948), 372.
Review of THE TELEPHONE at the Aldwych Theater
in London. The critic compares THE TELEPHONE's
score to Wolf-Ferrari's Segreto di Susanna. See
also THE MEDIUM.

Smith, Cecil. New Republic, CXVI (March 10, 1947), 40-41.
Short review. Smith sees the score as one of little
thought. Plot in a nutshell. See also THE
MEDIUM.

"Triple Bill at Sadler's Wells. " Musical Times, XCVIII (December, 1957), 679.
Review. Lucy and Ben are sung by June Bronhill
and Denis Dowling.

"Ventures in Lyric Theatre. " Theatre Arts, XXXI (May,
1947), 60-61.
Review at the Heckscher Theatre. THE TELE-
PHONE does not seem important. For this light
plot, Menotti has composed equally light music.
Its spontaneity is both its strength and weakness,
for the score seems more like an undisciplined first

draft than a finished work. Good plot summary.
Four paragraphs. See also THE MEDIUM.

Werker, G. "Utrechtse Opera-Belevenissen. " Mens en
    Melodie, VII (January, 1952), 7-8.
        Review of one large paragraph. Photo of Anneke
        van der Graaf and Frans van der Ven in THE
        TELEPHONE.

"The World of Music. " Etude, LXV (May, 1947), 294-295.
        Short review of the world premiere February 20.
        Marilyn Cotlow and Paul Kwartin sing excellently.
        Photo of Menotti.

Wyatt, Euphemia Van Rensselaer. Catholic World, CLXV
    (June, 1947), 265-266.
        Review. Wyatt is highly impressed. She thinks
        THE TELEPHONE needs a "lilting melody" to unify
        its elements. Two paragraphs. See also THE
        MEDIUM.

_____. _____, CLXXI (September, 1950), 469.
        Brief review at the Hotel Edison in New York.
        Edith Gordon sings Lucy. One paragraph. See
        also THE MEDIUM.

THE UNICORN, THE GORGON AND THE MANTICORE

Evett, Robert. "The Nail is 'it on the 'ead, Alors. " New
    Republic, CXXXV (October 29, 1956), 23.
        Review. The new work is "original" and expertly
        performed. Although it has characters and singers,
        it is not an opera but a cycle of madrigals. An
        audience of musicians and critics is enthusiastic.
        Evett says Menotti has become a "great composer"
        with this work.

Glock, William. London Musical Events, XIII (September,
    1958), 24-25.
        Review of a performance by the New Opera Com-
        pany and the Western Ballet Company at Sadler's
        Wells. Glock thinks the music is not very inventive
        with the low point being the march to the castle.
        But he has managed to make a text that projects
        well. It is a brilliant production. There are sug-
        gestions of Britten and Stravinsky. Menotti's

texture for differing situations is "imaginative. "
In one of the scenes between the Count and Countess
he has six vocal parts for the quick repartee.
Photos: A scene with the Western Ballet Company
and a rehearsal scene with Anne Hyde, Peter Darrell (choreographer), Laverne Meyer (Poet), Susanne Musitz (Countess) and Myer Fredman (conductor).

Krokover, Rosalyn. Musical Courier, CLV (February, 1957),
    47.
    Review of the New York City Ballet production.
    This is not a ballet or a madrigal but a fable.
    Krokover terms the performance and production
    superb. John Butler is the choreographer. The
    critic thinks the music is conservative in harmonics.
    Janet Reed dances the Countess. Other cast mem-
    bers are listed. Six paragraphs.

Levine, Joseph. "Gian Carlo Menotti: 'The Unicorn, the
    Gorgon and the Manticore, or The Three Sundays of
    a Poet. '" Music Library Association Notes, XV (De-
    cember, 1957), 144-145.
    Analysis. There is a cast of ten dancing charac-
    ters. Placement of chorus and dancers may vary.
    Menotti is interested in achieving an older sound
    with today's instruments. The form, twelve madri-
    gals, with alternating dance interludes is "original."
    Levine predicts less success for THE UNICORN
    than for earlier works. Good story summary.
    Seven paragraphs.

"Madrigal and Mime. " Time, LXVIII (November 5, 1956), 61.
    Review of the premiere Washington performance. It
    was commissioned by the Library of Congress.
    Menotti used as sources the madrigal cycles of
    Orazio Vecchi and The Book of Beasts. Five clos-
    ing lines for the chorus are quoted. The two open-
    ing performances for critics and general public are
    received with enthusiasm. Menotti would like the
    twelfth madrigal performed for his funeral. A foot-
    note defines the beasts. Plot summary for this
    forty-three minute work. Photos: Menotti, chore-
    ographer John Butler and the three dancers as the
    mythological creatures.

Mellen, Constance. "Beastes Among the Books. " Opera

News (December 3, 1956), 14.
Review of the premiere performance in the Coolidge
Auditorium at the Library of Congress. It is successful. Mellen provides a synopsis of the story.
There are symbolisms added to the simple tale.
Menotti's English text projects well. Vibrant costumes and "brilliant" dancing with mime are so
effective that the absence of even a backdrop is not
missed. An audience of many critics cheers the
premiere. Photos: The unicorn, gorgon, manticore, the poet and the count and countess. One
page.

"Messrs. Menotti and Rudel to the Fore. " Theatre Arts,
XLI (March, 1957), 823.
One paragraph review notice. This is one of
Menotti's finest works, warmly praised.

"New York City Ballet Gives Menotti Premiere. " Musical
America, LXXVII (February, 1957), 218.
Review of the New York premiere. The performance is praised in all aspects. The libretto and
music are the weaknesses; the result is a lack of
stylistic or artistic unity. The final passages fail
to convince this writer. He wonders if Menotti is
serious or tongue-in-cheek. But the dancers do
well and the audience is warmly receptive. Six
paragraphs.

Nordlinger, Genson, Jr. Musical Courier, CLIX (November
15, 1956), 21.
Short review of the first performance at the Twelfth
Festival of Chamber Music in the Library of Congress. The reviewer thinks it may have a chance
of staying in the repertory; it is a success.

"Novitaten. " Musica, XIII (June, 1959), 393.
Review of the first German performance at Han-
over's Wiener Staatsoper. Rudolf Hagelstange
translates the madrigals into German. Rudolf
Schulz designs the work poking fun at conventions
and with a sense of "roguishness. " Wolfgang
Trommer conducts. The cast of Horst Krause
(Poet), Bernard Weiss and Ursula Rieck (Couple),
Gregor Leue, Ralph Briegk and Richard Erwin is
mentioned. Yvonne Georgi is the choreographer.
Plot summary.

Potvin, Gilles. Canadian Music Journal, I (Summer, 1957),
    57, 59.
    Analytical article. Menotti contributes, not through
    reforms in opera, but by maintaining public interest
    in the theater. His style involves a "merger" of
    these composers: Puccini, Verdi, Strauss, Mus-
    sorgsky, Debussy and Berg. He has great talent in
    integrating a libretto with music. His forms--pre-
    lude, recitative, ensembles are "traditional" and the
    harmony "conventional. " He exhibits know-how in
    the use of the orchestra. THE UNICORN is sur-
    prising because of its looking back to the earliest
    days of opera in its material. Potvin finds like-
    nesses in Vecchi's L'Amfiparnaso and the UNICORN
    in their use of a cappella choruses. Some of the
    madrigals recall Monteverdi's style while in other
    sections Menotti uses more contemporary methods.
    There are suggestions of Stravinsky's L'Histoire du
    Soldat. While Vecchi said his L'Amfiparnaso was
    not for a visual "spectacle" Menotti uses dancers
    to show the action. Menotti starts with Vecchi's
    conception but goes beyond him in the visual side.
    Potvin believes the text is excellent, full of in-
    terest. THE UNICORN is for both the repertory of
    lyricism and choreography. Twelve paragraphs.

Rinaldi, Mario. "'L'Unicorno, la Gorgona e la Manticore'
    di Menotti. " Musica d'Oggi, III (June, 1960), 274.
    Review. The plot allows Menotti freedom in form.
    A ballet group from Hanover's Landestheater joins
    the orchestra of the Roman Philharmonic Academy.
    There are "sarcastic" aspects as in the madrigal of
    the 16th century. Wolfgang Trommer directs;
    Yvonne Georgi is the choreographer. It is a suc-
    cess.

Schaefer, Theodore. "Menotti's New Chamber Opera Given
    at Library of Congress. " Musical America, LXXVI
    (November 15, 1956), 6.
    Review. The fable exhilarates the audience.
    Schaefer describes the plot. He sees the madrigals
    as akin to Monteverdi's. He comments on the
    libretto, the Washington Chamber Chorus and the
    instruments. John Butler's choreography is "mem-
    orable. " All of the artists, conductor and com-
    poser are recalled many times for applause. Five
    paragraphs.

"So Menotti Beguiles. " <u>Newsweek</u>, XLVIII (November 5,
    1956), 79.
        Article. THE UNICORN charms with reminders of
        the sixteenth century Italian madrigal and the Japa-
        nese Kabuki.   Menotti explains his interest for
        works that small groups can perform.   The Eliza-
        beth Sprague Coolidge Foundation of the Library of
        Congress commissioned the work.   A footnote
        describes the three creatures from <u>The Book of
        Beasts</u>.   Brief plot summary.   Four paragraphs.

Terry, Walter.   <u>Saturday Review</u>, LV (May 27, 1972), 62.
        Review of a performance by the Cincinnati Ballet
        and the Cincinnati Symphony.   This production is
        from the Spoleto Festival with choreography by
        Louis Johnson.   The audience is enthusiastic at the
        Music Hall Auditorium.   Terry recalls John Butler's
        choreography as more effective.   But Terry likes
        the action "in movement" and the performances of
        Sharon Cole as the Countess and Orrin Kayan as
        the Poet.   To Terry it is "total lyric theater. "
        Four paragraphs.

"Twelfth Festival of Chamber Music. " <u>Pan Pipes</u>, XLIX
    (January, 1957), 15, 19.
        Review of the "opera" at the Library of Congress.
        It is a "madrigal opera. " Four lines describing the
        Poet are quoted.   The dying Poet's words, "Oh,
        foolish people... " are quoted.   Excerpts from Jay
        S. Harrison's October 22, 1956 review in the <u>New
        York Herald Tribune</u> about the instrumental inter-
        ludes.   He states they come from sixteenth century
        forms.   Harrison says it is an "inimitable Menotti
        product.... " Menotti is the stage director.   Plot
        summary in two short paragraphs.   Photos: Dying
        Man in the Castle (Swen Swenson), Count, Countess,
        Doctor, Doctor's Wife, Mayor, Mayor's Wife, Uni-
        corn, Gorgon and the Manticore.

V. GENERAL PERIODICAL ARTICLES

Ackart, Robert. "Opera Style All the While, But What Constitutes Style?" Musical America, LXXV (February 15, 1955), 22-23+.
Two paragraphs of lengthy article. Ackart says Menotti's characters are easy to recognize by the audience. Menotti's operas are not realistic in the sense of opera realism.

Aulicino, Armand. "In Defense of the Met." Theatre Arts, XXXVI (September, 1952), 74, 193.
THE MEDIUM is not suited for the Metropolitan Opera's size because of its intimacy. One paragraph. Photo of the composer.

Beyer, Henry. School and Society, LXXXI (September 16, 1950), 183-184.
Criticism of Menotti operas. Menotti has achieved much within imposed limitations. His style, form and treatment of music are eclectic in THE CONSUL. Once again he uses the macabre. The macabre in THE CONSUL's third dream is less moving. Patricia Neway makes the opera memorable. The cast is superb.

Bonvicini, Renzo. "L'Ultimo Menotti." La Scala, III (?) (June, 1952), 19-21.
Illustrated.

Bridge, Walter. "L' 'Opera' di Gian Carlo Menotti." Diapason (Milan), I (June-July, 1950), 9-11.

Briggs, John. "Menotti: Opera Magician." International Musician, LX (November, 1961), 12-13+.
Three interesting pages, mainly a history of the operas with some evaluation, their performances and critical reception. Toscanini's reaction to AMAHL is especially of interest. Photos: Menotti

117

Scott (Toby) in THE MEDIUM; THE CONSUL at the
State Opera in Ankara, Turkey; and Richard Cross
(Donato) and Franca Duval (Maria) in MARIA
GOLOVIN on NBC-TV.

"Broadway Gallery 1947-1948. " Harper's Bazaar, LXXXI
(October, 1947), 220.
Photo of Menotti.

Bruyr, Jose. "Gian-Carlo Menotti en Attendant 'Le Dernier
Sauvage.' " Le Guide du Concert et du Disque, CDI
(October, 1963), 4-5.
Biographical article. Bruyr points out the young
Menotti limped; his mother took him to the pil-
grimage of the Madonna del Monte. Much material
on AMAHL, THE CONSUL, THE SAINT, THE
TELEPHONE, THE UNICORN and THE LAST
SAVAGE. Menotti is fortunate in the excellent interpretations of Marie Powers in THE MEDIUM and
Patricia Neway in THE CONSUL. Although some
have associated him with Mussorgsky, Puccini,
Verdi and point to traces of Prokofieff, Strauss,
Debussy and Stravinsky, his work is "theater served
by the music. " In THE UNICORN Menotti shows a
remote succession to the Italian madrigalists, of
a capella ensemble and polyphonic writing. Quote
by Nicolas Slonimsky on Menotti's appeal to a large
public. Photo of Menotti working with an Amahl.

Butler, Henry. "A Measure of Menotti. " Opera News,
XXVIII (February 8, 1964), 26-27.
A director and librettist assess Menotti's operatic
production. Menotti has wanted his operas to be
known by a lay audience. He makes opera accessible by writing in a contemporary context. Butler
calls him an excellent storyteller. Menotti is
sensitive to how music works emotionally. His
emotional clearness is his trademark. He is a
perfectionist in theater detail. The composer admits his librettos are less than masterly.

"CBS and NBC Sponsor Contemporary Programs. " Musical
America, LXXII (May, 1952), 6.
Photo of Menotti with Milton Katims, William
Schuman and Howard Swanson.

Chotzinoff, Samuel. "The Guilt of Gian-Carlo Menotti. "

Holiday, XXXIII (June, 1963), 101-102+.

A conversation with Menotti on diverse matters. Most of the early part centers on the Spoleto Festival. After AMELIA at La Scala he becomes his own stage director. AMAHL assures him of a steady income. An enormous and lazy woman in Vienna inspires AMELIA which is his "good-luck piece." In THE ISLAND GOD, his study of German music comes forward. Menotti reveals his trick of telling the New York Times that he had "revised" THE MEDIUM. THE MEDIUM is the work which showed him what he was capable of doing. If necessary, he will sacrifice the libretto for the music. Much biographical material.

"Composer on Broadway." Time, LV (May 1, 1950), 64-66+.

Cover story article that discusses the Menotti career colorfully. Much detail about the composer's personal side, descriptions of his musical style and quotes from Menotti. Photos: Menotti rehearsing THE CONSUL; Marilyn Cotlow and Paul Kwartin in THE TELEPHONE; producers Zimbalist and Cowles; teacher Scalero and Puccini. Illustration of Menotti on the cover over "Composer Menotti His Opera is Vaaary Glooomy."

"Conductor and Composer." Musical Courier, CXV (April 17, 1937), 2.

Photo of Menotti and Fritz Reiner looking at the AMELIA score.

Eckertsen, Dean. "From Corelli to Menotti." Musical Journal, XIII (July-August, 1955), 13, 16.

Young American conductor compares and contrasts the music of two composers more than three centuries apart.

Edwards, Sydney. "Menotti Without Music." Music and Musicians, XIV (January, 1966), 17.

Interview article. Menotti charges young music critics oppose him. He will stop composing for a two year period. Edwards reminds Menotti of the public success THE LAST SAVAGE experienced at the Metropolitan Opera but the composer is unconvinced. He wants to "ruminate" now. Like Brahms and Rossini he wants to think on his future career.

Edwards speaks about a drive in New York City to
have a Menotti theatre.   Photo of Menotti with poet
Ezra Pound.

Ellsworth, Ray.   "Americans on Microgroove. "   High Fidelity,
VI (August, 1956), 62.
One paragraph is a summary of Menotti's operatic
output and his characteristics.   The second paragraph deals with the operas that have been recorded.

Evett, Robert.   "Trouble on Bleecker Street. "   Kenyon Review, XVII (Fall, 1965), 624-632.
Scholarly analysis of THE SAINT and his composing.   Menotti has made opera work in the commercial theater.   He grasps that Broadway is an
alternative to opera production.   His supervision of
THE MEDIUM gave a new authority to production.
He has been working toward opera for the same
audience as Tennessee Williams'.   One of his frus-
trations is how music can change the effect of
words, even meanings; another is what to do with
set pieces.   Some think his vocabulary becomes
"pedestrian" and too rough and the effect can be
unintentionally funny, but his music makes the
language expressive.   In THE SAINT he does not
make his stance apparent; he lets the ambiguities
add to the attraction.   Michele's opposition to Annina's entering a convent sustains the opera and
leads to much of its action.   An examination of
Menotti makes one wonder whether naturalistic opera
can be written without plot conventions such as Desideria's murder.   His music is a grand mixture.
The tradition he works in had practically disap-
peared before Puccini's death.   Why isn't Puccini
just as good an influence as other composers?
Evett discusses Menotti's use of melody, that he
gives more fully developed statements to instruments.   The Menotti orchestra departs from Puccini and many others; he exploits it and even lets
it dominate the singers.   In THE SAINT the music
is one of several styles.   For Menotti's work to
survive, Evett says he must give music a more
dominant role.   Now we need other composers who
have profited by Menotti's example to write opera
in English that will attract an audience.   Excellent
article.

"Gian-Carlo Menotti's Muziektheater. " Mens en Melodie, VII
  (February, 1952), 54-55.
    Included in the discussion are THE CONSUL and
    THE MEDIUM.   Profile photo of Menotti.   See also
    THE CONSUL.

Groth, Howard.   "Gian-Carlo Menotti and the American Lyric
    Theatre. " The Bulletin National Association of Teach-
    ers of Singing, XV (December, 1958), 16-17₊.
    Important critical article ranging from AMELIA to
    THE SAINT.   Groth's major views are for AMELIA,
    THE MEDIUM, THE TELEPHONE, THE CONSUL
    and AMAHL.   Groth closes with a quote from
    America's Music by Gilbert Chase.

Le Guide du Concert et du Disque, CD (October 26, 1963), 14.
    Left profile photo of Menotti.

Hijman, Julius.   "Menotti's Nieuwe Opera. " Mens en Melo-
    die, X (March, 1955), 77-79.
        Article.   Menotti and Aaron Copland cannot be com-
        pared.   To most of the public Copland is an "in-
        tellectual, " but Menotti has a large public.   Scho-
        enberg's son-in-law compares Menotti to Vicki
        Baum.   Hijman notes Menotti's claim in the New
        York Times that vocalism predates the spoken word.
        Hijman points to the "social tendencies" of Menotti's
        librettos pushing him to the fore of modern com-
        posers.   THE CONSUL is remembered as a "super-
        ior" score in which the dissonant and consonant
        are almost harmonious.   Hijman is disappointed in
        THE SAINT; it has no "problem. "   He believes
        THE SAINT's conflict is not very realistic and not
        well developed.   Menotti can be merely on the
        "periphery of reality, " as in the dancing of THE
        CONSUL.   The musical dissonants of THE SAINT
        are poor because they are not done with sophisti-
        cation and are easy to identify quickly.   This or-
        chestration is oriented more toward chords than to
        the voices.   Hijman finds the work "unorganized. "
        The score seems hastily done.   It has a heavy dis-
        advantage of being in the Verdi, Pizetti and Alfano
        style.   Photo of Menotti.

Hirsch, Nicole.   "Un Renovateur du Drame Lyrique: Gian-
    Carlo Menotti. " Musica (Chaix), XCIX (June, 1962),
    26-30.

Biographical article.   Menotti is not well known in
France.   THE CONSUL gave a rebirth to music
drama after World War II.   THE MEDIUM illustrates that Menotti is a man of the theater.   While
in Paris Menotti speaks little of his work but pre-
fers to talk about the Spoleto Festival.   He likes
the small town of Spoleto because there he feels
people see him as a "big brother."   His festival
has meant a resurgence to the town.   Against the
charge of making verismo Menotti states he thinks
his characters are "symbols" of contemporary society but not in a dark sense.   His revolution is to
put the lyric drama in today with characters who
are contemporary in their lives.   Menotti saw the
lyric drama as dying and losing its grip on the public.   An American influence is heavy on all of
Menotti's work.   He is undoubtedly one of the greatest directors of lyric drama.   Hirsch sees in his
stage direction a similarity to Fellini's films, a
"symbolic realism."   Hirsch describes his Spoleto
home overlooking the square of the Cathedral.   For
composing Menotti may go a thousand kilometers
from Spoleto looking for the right place of quiet.
He sometimes goes to the Italian Tyrol.   He enjoys
lengthy talks with friends on various projects.   He
is very involved in education such as his past teaching of composition at the Curtis Institute of Music
and courses at Spoleto for young singers.   Although
one can dislike the melodrama in his librettos, one
appreciates his untiring efforts to create.   Photos:
Menotti directing Denise Scharley as Mme. Flora at
the Opera-Comique and Denise Scharley (Mme.
Flora) and Marc Duchamp (Toby) in THE MEDIUM.

Hollander, Hans.   "Das Phanomen Gian-Carlo Menotti."
    Musik und Szene, III (?) (1958-1959), 65-67.
    Commentary.   Menotti's shorter works are his most
    famous; they are unusually original.   He deals with
    psychological and social problems and symbolic at-
    mospheres.   Menotti's operas have the modern
    music drama about them as well as the operatic
    aestheticism.   His influences include Schoenberg,
    Berg, Busoni, Hindemith, Janacek and many re-
    minders of Puccini.   He has an uncanny sense for
    the theatrical and realistic for a balance of music
    and drama.   Other well developed senses are his
    realization of a scene's atmosphere, his use of

economy, buildups and the turmoil of emotions.
Photo of Menotti.

"In the News. " Opera, XXII (September, 1971), 778.
Menotti's excerpted thoughts on nudity in opera,
opera houses and the future of opera.

"Inside Stuff. " Variety, XLXXXVII (January 18, 1955), 72.
Excerpts from Menotti's article on opera as theatre
in the New York Times.

Kanski, Jozef. "Gian Carlo Menotti w Warszawie. " Ruch
Muzyczny, XVI (n. 4, 1972), 6-7.
Interview in association with THE CONSUL in War-
saw. An example of Menotti's handwriting. Photos:
Menotti and a press conference with Zdzistaw
Sliwinski, Antoni Wicherek and Andrzej Sadowski.

Kay, Norman. "Menotti: Operatic Master. " Music and
Musicians, XV (March, 1967), 28-31.
Good article. Kay discusses whether he is an
"original" composer. Why should influences be used
as negative criticism of Menotti? Menotti is the
natural musician. AMELIA is a traditional opera
buffa of the vernacular; Menotti found an effective
way to work common English conversation and prose
into opera. In AMELIA the Italian libretto influences the work's phrasing. THE OLD MAID is in
the American vernacular aided by his "unembar-
rassed fascination" for English. Again like
AMELIA the plot is a nonsensical one. Here he is
conservative and uses music thus so to convey do-
mestic talk. In THE MEDIUM most noticeable is
his new flexibility; stress and pace become more
important. His music for Mme. Flora is markedly
different, more declamatory and jagged. THE
TELEPHONE returns to opera buffa. Menotti's
chief interest in this light work may be the situation
and suitable language. THE CONSUL is his most
"consistent" work. Menotti exploits religion and
pathos in AMAHL. THE SAINT must be considered
along with its religious background. The musical
motifs of Michele and Annina mingle in the secret
meeting scene most effectively. One's temperament
will influence how THE SAINT is accepted. His
style is here more difficult to accept because of his
exposed temperament. The music of THE DEATH

OF THE BISHOP OF BRINDISI echoes that of THE
SAINT. THE CONSUL is neither "opera" nor
"drama." Certainly it is not a "musical."
AMAHL in form could be used for an "English
children's Christmas pantomime." His point of view
is a child's, but the simple story has many larger
things to say. It is a universal story. As in the
reserve used for the story, the music has a concentration on basics. Although there are devices
of Christmas carol and folk music, the harmonics
are colder. A Puccini influence remains though less
so than earlier. For its theatrical combining of
elements, AMAHL is the best example of the Menotti
form. Brief plot summaries. Photos: Profile of
the composer; 1957 production of THE TELEPHONE
at Sadler's Wells with June Bronhill and Denis
Dowling; THE CONSUL at Sadler's Wells with Amy
Shuard as Magda.

Kolodin, Irving. "The Cloak Uncovers Menotti." Saturday
    Review, XXXV (March 1, 1952), 25.
        Kolodin sees in Puccini's Il Tabarro a considerable
        influence on Menotti's style of composing.

_____. "From 'Amelia' to 'The Saint.'" Saturday Re-
    view, XXXVIII (January 29, 1955), 37-38.
        An appearance of an Angel recording of AMELIA
        leads Kolodin to a scholarly look at Menotti's de-
        velopment as a composer. Kolodin has such sensible
        and sensitive insights that this article is excellent
        for any examination of Menotti.

Kubly, Herbert. "Chamber of Horrors in Capricorn."
    Theatre Arts, XXXIII (January, 1949), 32-35.
        Interesting facts about his life and personality along
        with information on the operas from THE DEATH
        OF PIERROT to THE CONSUL.

Lansdale, Nelson. "Menotti Calls The Met a Museum."
    Theatre Arts, XXXVI (May, 1952), 30-31+.
        Menotti argues that the Metropolitan Opera has an
        obligation to present contemporary opera. Menotti
        mentions daring managerial enterprises in Paris
        with THE CONSUL and at La Scala with the same
        work.

Lillich, Meredith. "Menotti's Music Dramas." Educational

Theatre Journal, XI (December, 1959), 271-279.
Excellent discussion of the relative place and worth
of music and drama in Menotti and the joining of
libretto and music. Menotti's "form" displays a
rare unity, much more than the usual opera production. Taken separately, his music and plots show
weaknesses. Menotti is an excellent librettist. His
libretti deal with the basics of love, hate, blood,
death, and the like. Since his music is so eclectic,
Puccini is often mentioned in discussions about him;
he is not often atonal. While Menotti intends THE
MEDIUM to be a philosophical work, his libretto
fails to support this because the style is not distinguished. Generally, critics are favorable toward
THE MEDIUM's music. Some admire his lyricism
for perfunctory dialogue while others associate such
composition with the Puccini school and Mascagni
and Leoncavallo. Despite THE CONSUL's emotional
nature, the libretto is not strong enough to stand
alone. This work's immediacy allows Menotti to
further his liking of melodrama. His characterizations of the Magician, the Lady, the Elderly Gentle-
man and, most particularly, the Secretary, are not
banal. The irony is that the Secretary, the Consul
and bureaucracy become unintentional villains. In
THE CONSUL the story leads; in THE SAINT this
"form" is sometimes evident but no longer practical
theatrically. It belongs in the opera house because
of its larger size. The source for THE SAINT
comes from his early life. In the faith versus
reason struggle, the solution is not resolved and
some feel Menotti is unsure of his theme here.
His text has aroused varying criticisms. In THE
SAINT perhaps he has overlooked logic too much
for theatrical impact. Its music is also confused.
There is a fine balance between music and drama
as set pieces advance the story. THE SAINT departs from the chamber-opera form and is grand
opera. Menotti has attempted to give opera a new
form which is not conventional. Perhaps his form
is practical only for him. While he veers more
toward drama, Broadway musicals have seemed
more operatic.

Maione, Rino. "Critica a Menotti." La Scala, CXXXIX
(June, 1961), 14-17.
Critical commentary. Photos of Menotti directing

a rehearsal of THE SAINT at La Scala, THE CON-
SUL at the Barrymore Theatre, Franca Duval and
Richard Cross in MARIA and Gabriella Ruggiero and
Eugenia Ratti (Carmela) in THE SAINT.

Mellers, Wilfrid. "Music Theatre and Commerce: A Note on
Greshwin, Menotti and Marc Blitzstein. " Score, XII
(June, 1955), 71.
Composer Mellers compares Menotti with Gershwin.
Unlike Gershwin's music though, he says Menotti's
lacks identity. One paragraph.

Menotti, Gian-Carlo. High Fidelity/Musical America, XX
(March, 1970), 7, Section 2.
Menotti's thoughts excerpted from the City Center
Playbill. His comments on nudity in opera, AMAHL's
message for his generation and HELP! HELP! THE
GLOBOLINKS's for the "new generation. "

_____. "I Am the Savage. " Opera News, XXVIII (Feb-
ruary 8, 1964), 8-12.
Revealing article. THE LAST SAVAGE comes from
Menotti's thoughts over a period of time. The influences of civilization are treated in several of
Menotti's operas. Opera buffa is music of joy. In
the best opera buffa the music itself is laughter.
Even if there are no "supermen, " there are still
"savages. " Each of Menotti's operas is autobio-
graphical, obvious or otherwise. There is no set
formula for effective opera. Opera buffa treats
human weaknesses. As theater opera needs less of
the preconceived. Contemporary opera is indeed a
departure from past opera. It is difficult to stage
opera for favorable comparison with plays. Even
though he is often frustrated with singer's desire
only to sing rather than act, he would not leave
music. Photos: Full page profile of Menotti; Chet
Allen, the first Amahl; Poleri toasting DiGerlando
and Aiken in THE SAINT: Neway in THE CONSUL;
John Reardon and Judith Raskin in water in
LABYRINTH; Frances Yeend and Walter Cassel in
AMELIA; and Marie Powers breaking up her seance
while Monica comforts Toby in THE MEDIUM.

_____. "Notes on Opera as Basic Theatre. " New York
Times Magazine, CIV (January 2, 1955), 11, 23.
Article that states Menotti's basic beliefs about

opera as theater and that song is more immediate
than the spoken word. Opera is the very basis of
theatre. Dramas were sung before they were
spoken. Great operas will outlive plays of the
same period. For example, compare the lasting
power of a good Verdi opera and a good Victor Hugo
play. The fault of contemporary opera lies with
music that fails to communicate. Every language
can be used for opera. There are great advantages
in the use of translations, even if some subtleties
are lost.

_____. "Notes on Opera as Basic Theater. " Perspectives
USA, XII (Summer, 1955), 5-9.
Specific references to THE CONSUL and THE SAINT
in the paragraph on translation problems.

_____. "Opera Isn't Dead. " Etude, LXVIII (February,
1950), 14-15₊.
Early article expressing Menotti's belief in opera's
vitality and staying power. Specific references to
his operas concern THE OLD MAID and THE TELE-
PHONE. Menotti composes his libretto and music
simultaneously. Menotti finds some young singers
very flexible. Photos: Menotti; the final scene of
THE MEDIUM with Marie Powers and Leo Coleman; and Powers (Miss Todd) and Ellen Faull (Miss
Pinkerton) in THE OLD MAID at the New York City
Opera.

_____. "A Plea for the Creative Artist. " New York
Times Magazine (June 29, 1952), 8, 22-23.
Substantial article. Menotti contends Americans
have little value for the composer, the creator.
Americans appreciate the interpreters much more.
Photo of Menotti directing AMAHL.

_____. "A Point of Contact. " Opera News, XXXIV (De-
cember 27, 1969), 8-11.
Three page article discussing problems of reaching
the American public. Menotti says opera in the
United States is still a foreign bird. In one paragraph he cites the large public for THE MEDIUM,
THE CONSUL and AMAHL.

_____. "Reflections on Opera Buffa. " National Music
Council Bulletin, XXIV (Winter, 1963-1964), 18.

Mainly opera buffa.   Three brief paragraphs on
THE LAST SAVAGE, its humor.

"Menotti Auditions London Boy Singers. " Musical Events,
XIX (April, 1964), 11.
Photo of Menotti auditioning a boys' choir for
MARTIN'S LIE.

"Menotti Dossier. " Vogue, CXXV (March, 1955), 143-145+.
Entertaining biographical article.   Forty million see
the wedding scene from THE SAINT on television's
"Toast of the Town. "   The best features are the
twenty-two photographs, many not often used.
Photos: Theresa Neumann of Bavaria with stigmata;
miniature of his mother; his score for THE DEATH
OF PIERROT; Japanese production of THE OLD
MAID; Marie Powers as Mme. Flora peering into a
mirror; the composer taking a curtain call at La
Scala after THE CONSUL; Menotti looking through a
phrenology chart, photos and memorabilia on the
wall of his study; full page photo of Gabriella Ruggiero (Annina) praying with the dying Gloria Lane
(Desideria) in THE SAINT.

"Menotti Mania. " Opera News, XVI (October 29, 1951), 18-
19.
In 1951 there are 357 performances of Menotti
operas in the United States.   Photos: THE CONSUL,
THE MEDIUM, THE TELEPHONE and THE OLD
MAID.

"Midsummer Applause. " Harper's Bazaar, LXXX (July,
1946), 87.
Photo of Menotti with a MEDIUM prop, a phrenology
chart.

"Names. " Opera News, XXVI (May 5, 1962), 4.
Photo of Menotti with soprano Gabriella Tucci.

"Names, Dates & Places. " Opera News, XXXIV (December
20, 1969), 5.
Photo of Menotti.

"Opera's Heir Presumptive. " Newsweek, XXXV (March 27,
1950), 82-83.
Interesting article about Menotti's accomplishments.
Menotti may become our first important opera com-

poser. Only THE ISLAND GOD has been a failure.
THE CONSUL is his most acclaimed. Plot summary of this opera. Patricia Neway, Gloria Lane
and Marie Powers are outstanding in their roles in
THE CONSUL. Menotti and Puccini share similarities. Menotti keeps his common sense despite his
successes, realizing how damaging a flop can be.
Photo of Patricia Neway, Marie Powers and the
police in THE CONSUL.

Parinaud, Andre. "Io sono l'Ultimo Selvaggio. " Musica
  d'Oggi, VI (n. 5, 1963), 262-265.
    Interview for Arts translated into Italian. Menotti
    believes THE LAST SAVAGE is his "most coura-
    geous" opera since he tries to leave contemporary
    music completely in it. He has attempted to em-
    phasize "grace" and "softness" and to avoid a com-
    plex language. Menotti explains the story of THE
    LAST SAVAGE. This story represents, as always
    some of Menotti's self, his own yearning for a
    primitive life. MARIA GOLOVIN concerns a Menotti
    weakness, jealousy. He admires Puccini and Mus-
    sorgsky but has the greatest affinity for Schubert.
    To him critics are too concerned with possible
    "revolutionaries. " He dislikes the current craze for
    the "arbitrary and eccentric. " As an older composer,
    he works in the morning. He dislikes recordings and
    calls their sounds "unnatural. " His standing in Italy
    has gone from the negative controversy around THE
    CONSUL to a more tempered climate in later years.
    He expresses regret over life's brevity; there is a de-
    sire to have done many things left undone. The "Don
    Giovanni" character repulses him. To himself he is
    not a "romantic," more of a mystic. In a credo state-
    ment, he says art is not a "process of invention but
    of discovery. " It involves memory and discovery,
    an inevitability which can be found through research.
    Every artist has ambitions to have his work survive.
    The public is the same in different ages.

_____. "S Giancerlem Menottim. " Hudebni Rozhledy,
    XVII (n. 3, 1964), 122-123.
    Interview.

"Pas de Surhomme: un Medium. " Musica (Chaix), XCVII
    (April, 1962), 10.
      Short article. Georges Hirsch of the Opera had

commissioned an opera from Menotti several years
ago. Late last year the Opera of Marseille did THE
MEDIUM. Then Louis Ducreux took this cast for
the Salle Favart, its first performance there.

"Personalities and Events of the Week." Illustrated London
News, CCXXVI (May 14, 1955), 885.
Photo of Menotti due to his 1955 Pulitzer Prixe for
THE SAINT.

Pinzauti, Leonardo. "A Colloquio con Gian Carlo Menotti."
Rivista Musicale Italiana, IV (July-August, 1970), 717-
720.
Interview. He considers himself "out of fashion."
He retains the same distaste for much of twentieth
century music. To him art is researching the "inevitable," not discovering the new. Beautiful melodies remind us perhaps of the inevitable. Art
refers to "eternal factors" and therefore aesthetic-
ally it does not progress. Central to art is re-
membering. Art involves expressions inside a
"game" and a form. The fugue and sonnet survive
because they are open to many different forms of
expression. Art requires a transforming of elements; without the transforming, the music might
remain folkloric. A composer must be able to
place himself in the place of other listeners as well
as using his own ears. His writing is not to please
the public. He calls the polemics of Zdanov's
followers "ridiculous." There is no longer a real
public because it is afraid to declare itself. He
admires Boulez as an interpreter but says his
writings are pretentious. Critics again have made
the mistake of considering Boulez, like Schoenberg,
an outstanding intellectual. It is hard to explain
why great melodies work, but the composer's "di-
vining rod" has succeeded. Wagner knew this at
the start of Die Meistersinger. If Menotti were
born today, he would compose simple "monody."
Since the young do not understand the realities of
themselves, music may continue to be accessible
only as a language to musicians. As a skeptic he
has a great admiration for Voltaire. In Stravinsky
he is pleased most by the music of the Les Noces
period. He defends Gesualdo a Orlando di Lasso
as a great artist, despite his lack of performance
today. Among his influences are Scarlatti, Schubert

and for his operas, Mussorgsky. In Puccini he
admires his "singing speech" much more than the
music. He has written more operas than other
forms of music, partly out of fate since after his
first work there were many requests for more. The
"dynamic function" of dissonance has been crushed
by modern music. His hobbies are "secret ambi-
tions" and reading before bedtime. He has no plans
of moving to Italy in retirement. If he were re-
born, there would not be another Spoleto. He is a
"skeptic with enthusiasm. " Photo of Menotti watching performers at Spoleto.

"Radio Poll Winners Accept Their Awards. " Musical America, LXXII (July, 1952), 4.
Photo of Menotti with Samuel Chotzinoff. AMAHL
wins "Best New Work of Any Type. "

Rizzo, Francis. "Diary of Two Deadlines. " Opera News,
XXXV (March 13, 1971), 268.
An associate of Menotti (American manager of the
Spoleto Festival from 1968 to 1970) describes
Menotti's frenetic days in January, 1971, as he
supervises the French premiere at Marseilles of
the revised MARIA GOLOVIN and composes THE
MOST IMPORTANT MAN. Written with excitement
and immediacy.

Rosenwald. Hans. Music News XLIII (April, 1951), 11.
One substantial paragraph of commentary. Rosenwald calls him the "most important composer of
opera of the younger generation. "

Sargeant, Winthrop. 'Imperishable Menotti. " New Yorker,
XXXVI (February 27, 1960), 133-135.
Sargeant comments on his operatic output. He says
his gift is knowing how to write opera, the intuition
of realizing what drama is suitable for opera. See
also THE CONSUL.

_____. "On Opera. " New Yorker, XXX (January 22,
1955), 77.
Thoughts with relation to THE SAINT on the importance of drama versus music in opera.

_____. "Orlando in Mount Kisco. " New Yorker, XXXIX
(May 4, 1963), 49-50+.

Very extensive and valuable article. Sargeant begins by discussing Menotti's "standing apartness."
He is extremely individual. He thinks of himself
as an American composer and is very concerned
with communicating to the public. Sargeant rates
three operas, THE MEDIUM, THE CONSUL and
AMAHL as masterpieces. For his popularity, some
highbrow critics have called him an old-fashioned
sentimentalist. But Menotti is very much a contemporary composer. Sargeant analyzes reasons
for his success and indicates that composers such
as Douglas Moore and Carlisle Floyd have been
stimulated by him. Part of Menotti's creed is that
eccentricity and exoticism have been overemphasized
to distinguish one's personal trademark in art. To
him the basic means of appealing to an audience
have not changed. The element of illusion is very
important. His "heroes" are feminine characters.
The tragedy-comedy element is essential to opera.
Then Sargeant writes about the personal Menotti and
his home at Mt. Kisco. (In his home are a self-
portrait of the young woman who inspired THE
SAINT and the knight figure of Orlando). Sargeant
provides much detail of Menotti's early life in Italy
and his period with Rosario Scalero at the Curtis
Institute of Music. A large Viennese baroness is
the inspiration for the aristocratic woman of
AMELIA. He is suddenly famous. AMELIA and
THE OLD MAID fall in the long Italian tradition of
opera buffa. The failure of THE ISLAND GOD
which has never been published leads the composer
to question what type of operatic drama he should
compose. THE MEDIUM becomes a classic. Sargeant says it has all of the parts that have become
identified with him. The next period is in Hollywood. THE CONSUL is his first "long work."
Sargeant describes the plot briefly, the inspiration
for the basic idea and other pertinent facts of its
history. THE CONSUL's premiere at La Scala
serves to illustrate a partially humorous reaction
by a Milan critic and other biographical episodes in
Italy. AMAHL strikes a claim toward operatic im-
mortality. THE SAINT is not a large success.
Sargeant discusses reasons for this. For one thing
piety is not dramatically powerful. Menotti starts
his administration of the Spoleto Festival. During
this period only MARIA GOLOVIN is completed.

Sargeant examines the television opera, LABY-
RINTH, and the comedy, THE LAST SAVAGE. The
excellent article is concluded with a look at his
originality and current popularity and his faith in
opera's unique staying power. He is the rare "pro-
fessional composer. " Opera can make bad drama
acceptable, even good.   With a sketch of Menotti.

_____. "Wizard of the Opera. " Life, XXVIII (May 1,
     1950), 81-82+.
     Another well-written Sargeant article.   Despite its
     awards by drama critics, THE CONSUL is opera.
     THE CONSUL illustrates contemporary opera can
     be vital.   Sargeant terms it "first class" giving
     reasons.   So great was his concern over THE CON-
     SUL Menotti suffered a nervous collapse.   He hopes
     THE CONSUL will not have a long run to prevent
     staleness.   His experience with failure is small.
     Sargeant writes considerably about his personal life.
     AMELIA runs for two seasons at the Metropolitan
     Opera.   THE ISLAND GOD's failure is an important
     lesson on too much profundity in opera.   THE
     MEDIUM is also very serious, but it has real the-
     atrical impact.   Menotti dislikes the sophisticated
     dissonance of his contemporaries.   His gift of sin-
     cere sentiment and his originality of operatic style
     plus other factors may be the operatic wave to go
     with modern theatrical trends.   Photos: Menotti
     composing, the eleven-year-old boy carrying his
     sister's bridal train and the composer with his dog
     outside his home.

Samuel, Claude.   "Sauvage Mais Idealiste.... " Le Guide du
     Concert et du Disque, CDIII (November 2, 1963), 8.
     Interview on modern music for the Tribune de la
     Musique Vivante.   Menotti says he was educated in
     the German school, making it normal to dislike
     opera.   The idea for his first opera came from a
     lady's dressing table in Vienna.   He thinks reasons
     for his successes are the simple language and
     musical clarity.   He says modern music is the
     "love of one's self. "   Other contemporaries use a
     "beautiful language which is not colloquial. " Menotti
     is concerned with writing good recitative.   He be-
     came a stage director in reaction to the older
     "sergeants. "   The text is not more important than
     the music. The Spoleto Festival represents Menotti's

search for making the artist necessary as in the
Renaissance.

Taubman, Howard. "Gian-Carlo Menotti. " Theatre Arts,
    XXXV (September, 1951), 26-27₊.
        Substantial article about Menotti's career. He is
        the most successful opera composer since Puccini,
        but he remains humble about his successes as his
        friends predicted. He proves that operas can be
        successful in English and that they can treat con-
        temporary topics. Broadway calls his operas
        "music dramas. " Music will speak universally when
        other forms fail, he believes. His versatility is
        illustrated by his complete supervision of his works.
        For example, he was the director the THE MED-
        IUM film. In his composing he works intensely for
        ten to fifteen minutes and then breaks, a pattern he
        can continue for hours. His composing started
        seriously when he was sixteen. For his first opera
        as an adult he wrote the libretto first in Italian be-
        fore translating. In AMELIA he uses his experi-
        ences as he usually does. THE MEDIUM proves he
        would not repeat the mistake of THE ISLAND GOD.
        THE CONSUL's theme is a noble one. Magda's
        aria, "To this we've come, " illustrates Menotti's
        belief in permanent values. Menotti thinks the
        public has better taste than it realizes. He would
        like more recognition in Italy. At La Scala THE
        CONSUL causes violent demonstrations. Toscanini
        has befriended him. The great conductor surprised
        him by attending the openings of THE TELEPHONE
        and THE MEDIUM. Toscanini shows a high regard
        for THE CONSUL by his reaction. Photo of Menotti
        looking at himself in a dressing room mirror.

_____. "A Prodigy Grows Up. " New York Times Maga-
    zine (June 1, 1947), 28.
        Perceptive article by the critic.

_____. "Proving Opera Can Be Modern. " New York
    Times Magazine (March 19, 1950), 26-30.
        Extensive article. THE CONSUL makes for a better
        future for musical comedy. Opera remains a rarity
        on Broadway. One grateful woman admits how
        moved she is yet implies that THE CONSUL is not
        an opera. At a bar after a performance, the hat-
        check girl has been so touched by THE CONSUL

that she requests the drinks be free. Toscanini
shows obvious high regard for the work. Menotti
makes words that are effectively sung. The writer
questions the composer about what music adds to a
narrative. Menotti says great melodies bring forth
a universal response. He composes music and text
simultaneously. He remembers how various sections of THE CONSUL came to him. One cannot
divide words and music so dependent as they are
upon each other. He delights in English as song.
As an Italian, English to him is "exotic." Because
of production problems in opera, he wants to be the
stage director. The composer knows what he wants
from his cast and therefore is unusually precise.
He had an early yearning for the stage. AMELIA
clearly reflects the Italian opera buffa tradition.
THE OLD MAID is his first completely American
subject. THE ISLAND GOD proves to be a mistake.
Menotti thinks he errs in treating a theme too phil-
osophically. He says one must write always to the
emotions and let the philosophy be an inner part of
the work. Menotti finds an even larger public for
THE MEDIUM. He writes for absolutely everyone.
The MEDIUM's great success on Broadway opens the
way for other composers. Photos: Marie Powers,
Patricia Neway, Leon Lishner and the police in
THE CONSUL; AMELIA and THE ISLAND GOD at
the Metropolitan Opera; Marie Powers in THE
MEDIUM; Menotti; Marilyn Cotlow and Frank Rogier
in THE TELEPHONE and Marie Powers and Ellen
Faull in THE OLD MAID.

Taylor, William A. "Menotti Tells about His Video Opera
    Commissioned by NBC-TV." Musical Courier,
    CXXXIX (May 1, 1949), 8.
        Article about Menotti's plans for the work that be-
        comes AMAHL. At this point the work is to be
        called IRENE AND THE GYPSIES. It will be a
        fantasy, a mother's search for her lost child.
        Menotti says operas as created for the stage will
        not work on television. Photo of Menotti.

Todd, Arthur. "Theatre on the Disk." Theatre Arts, XXXVI
    (June, 1952), 7.
        Review of the operas that have been recorded. Dis-
        cussed are AMAHL (RCA Victor), THE CONSUL
        (Decca), THE MEDIUM and THE TELEPHONE (Co-

lumbia), the sound track of THE MEDIUM film
(Mercury), AMELIA (RCA Victor, then unavailable)
and THE OLD MAID (Cetra, then unavailable).

Yarustovsky, Boris. Journal of Research in Music Education,
    X (Fall, 1962), 125.
    One paragraph of commentary.

VI. NEWSPAPER ARTICLES
(by Opera)

AMAHL AND THE NIGHT VISITORS

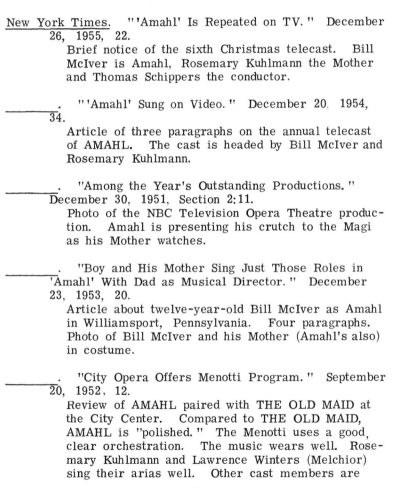

New York Times. "'Amahl' Is Repeated on TV. " December
26, 1955, 22.
Brief notice of the sixth Christmas telecast. Bill
McIver is Amahl, Rosemary Kuhlmann the Mother
and Thomas Schippers the conductor.

_____. "'Amahl' Sung on Video. " December 20, 1954,
34.
Article of three paragraphs on the annual telecast
of AMAHL. The cast is headed by Bill McIver and
Rosemary Kuhlmann.

_____. "Among the Year's Outstanding Productions. "
December 30, 1951, Section 2:11.
Photo of the NBC Television Opera Theatre production. Amahl is presenting his crutch to the Magi
as his Mother watches.

_____. "Boy and His Mother Sing Just Those Roles in
'Amahl' With Dad as Musical Director. " December
23, 1953, 20.
Article about twelve-year-old Bill McIver as Amahl
in Williamsport, Pennsylvania. Four paragraphs.
Photo of Bill McIver and his Mother (Amahl's also)
in costume.

_____. "City Opera Offers Menotti Program. " September
20, 1952, 12.
Review of AMAHL paired with THE OLD MAID at
the City Center. Compared to THE OLD MAID,
AMAHL is "polished. " The Menotti uses a good,
clear orchestration. The music wears well. Rosemary Kuhlmann and Lawrence Winters (Melchior)
sing their arias well. Other cast members are

mentioned. Nine paragraphs. See also THE OLD
MAID.

_____. "City Opera Offers Menotti Twin Bill. " March
23, 1953, 27.
Brief paragraph on AMAHL at the City Center.
James Sammarco is Amahl. See also THE MED-
IUM.

_____. Downes, Olin. "City Opera Offers Menotti's
'Amahl.'" April 10, 1952, 36.
Review of the first stage performance of AMAHL at
the City Center by the New York City Opera paired
with THE OLD MAID. Downes praises the performance. He believes it gains through the stage
over its strengths on television. Chet Allen again
is the stellar star as Amahl. All of the Magi are
singled out for their vocal interpretations. The
dancers are outstanding. Thomas Schippers' debut
as conductor is "perceptive. " Eight paragraphs.
See also THE OLD MAID.

_____. Downes, Olin. "Menotti's 'Amahl' is a Historic
Step in the Development of a New Idiom. " December,
30, 1951, Section 2:7.
Lengthy review of AMAHL, its television premiere.
AMAHL is the first opera composed specifically for
television. Discussed are the limitations of television for opera and the story with an explanation
of the genesis of AMAHL. Additional paragraphs on
the work's proportion, the choreography the
Mother's passage in which she sings "All that gold,"
and the performance of Chet Allen in the title role.
Around two columns. Important article for the
serious student.

_____. Downes, Olin. "Menotti-Opera, the First for TV,
Has Its Premiere; Boy, 12, Is Star. " December 25,
1951, 1, 38.
Front page review of the first television performance
in Radio City's Studio H-8. Downes finds it very
moving. He gives the story briefly and explains the
inspiration for the composer, the Bosch painting.
Twelve-year-old Chet Allen is praised for his Amahl.
His performance does not seem like a lesson learned
well but the natural behavior and feeling of a young
boy. Menotti's way of fitting his creation to the new

medium speaks highly of his talents in musical theatre. Throughout, the music meets the required
drama with beauty for climaxes. For the choruses
of the shepherds and other ensembles Menotti has
written poetic music that is not commonplace.
Downes says the Three Kings and the Servant are
admirable performers. Menotti's childhood is used
for the reason behind Caspar's deafness. Rosemary
Kuhlmann as the Mother is "moving." Downes believes the production is ahead of television's resources. Downes witnesses an epochal event in
television history. Fourteen paragraphs. Photos
of Amahl and his Mother and the Shepherds bearing
gifts.

_____. "Film 'Quo Vadis' Wins Five Christopher Prizes."
February 15, 1952, 17.
Article. NBC wins a $3,000 Christopher Award for
AMAHL. The award is divided between Menotti,
producer Samuel Chotzinoff and director Kirk
Browning.

_____. Henahan, Donal. "'Amahl' and 'Globolinks' Per-
formed." December 24, 1970, 10.
Review of AMAHL billed with HELP! HELP! at the
ANTA Theater. Henahan apparently feels AMAHL
is suitable mainly during the Christmas season.
Robert Puleo does well as Amahl and Nancy Williams makes a character out of the Mother. David
Clatworthy (Melchior), Edward Pierson (Balthazar)
and Douglas Perry (Kaspar) are effective performers as is Joseph Galiano (Page). But Henahan finds
this AMAHL production "vulgar" and "cosmetic."
Menotti stages; Christopher Keene conducts. Three
paragraphs. See also HELP! HELP!

_____. Hughes, Allen. "Miss Somogi Leads 'Amahl' First
Time." December 26, 1970, 11.
Review of AMAHL at the ANTA conducted by Judith
Somogi in her Broadway conducting debut. Hughes
likes her choice of tempo and the balance between
voices and orchestra. Four short paragraphs.

_____. Louchheim, Aline B. "Television Opera and the
Artist." December 30, 1951, Section 2: 9.
Article about scenic designer Eugene Berman's work
for AMAHL. Visually AMAHL is disappointing.

Berman wanted to depict AMAHL's timeless quality.
His preliminary drawings had no relation to practical problems of television production.   Berman
realized a television camera is more penetrating
and requires detailed realism.   His idea of warped
wood sets ends up as painted canvas which is ex-
actly the impression this viewer received.   While
the set looked "beautiful" at rehearsal, the colors
of the background and the costumes became too alike
on screen.   Louchheim questions why there was a
need to depict realism visually.   She suggests that
the settings were not adequately adjusted to the
medium.   Illustration of Berman's "original idea"
for the setting.   Eight paragraphs.

_____.   "Menotti Writing an Opera for TV. "   November
8,   1951,   31.
Article about Menotti's commission from NBC to
write an opera "expressly for television. "   He will
receive $5, 000.   This work has been described as
a "miracle play. "   Amahl is for a boy of twelve.
Seven paragraphs.

_____.   "Music: Premiere of One-Act Opera. "   April 2,
1954,   24.
Notice.   Cast and production credits for AMAHL at
the City Center.   William McIver (Amahl) makes
his debut.

_____.   "NBC Weighs Repeat of Menotti TV Opera. "   De-
cember 26,   1951,   30.
Article of six short paragraphs.   After the premiere
telecast, listeners call the NBC switchboard for over
an hour in their praise.   Public response to the
opera has been very favorable.

_____.   "New 'Amahl' Is Seen In Opera on NBC-TV. "
December 26, 1963, 36.
Review of a new AMAHL production by the NBC
Opera Company.   New is Kurt Yaghjian as Amahl.
It shines more than in the past.   Others in the cast
are Martha King, Richard Cross, Willis Patterson
and Julian Patrick.   Donald MacKayle and dancers
perform.   Five short paragraphs.

_____.   "New 'Amahl' Seen on TV. "   December 25, 1956,
30.

Review of the annual AMAHL telecast. Kirk
Jordan, ten, is the new Amahl. His voice is good
except for the highest notes. Robert Montgomery
introduces the work. Four short paragraphs.

_____. "Radio and TV Cited in Peabody Awards." May 2,
1952, 27.
Article. AMAHL wins a George Foster Peabody
Award for 1951.

_____. "Schippers Leads Menotti Program." August 1,
1952, 9.
Review of a Lewisohn Stadium concert. Rosemary
Kuhlmann and Richard Mincer sing the first scene
of AMAHL. Brief comments on the opera. Thomas
Schippers gives excellent conducting. See also
AMELIA and THE ISLAND GOD.

_____. Schonberg, Harold C. "Opera: Two by Menotti."
December 23, 1969, 21.
Brief notice of AMAHL on a double bill with HELP!
at the City Center. Robert Puleo sings Amahl.
With cast and production credits. See also HELP!
HELP!

_____. Sullivan, Dan. "'Amahl' Is Out of NBC Christ-
mas List." September 23, 1966, 74.
Article. AMAHL will not be shown on NBC Television this coming Christmas because the network
has refused to tape a new production. Menotti describes the 1963 taping with Kurt Yaghjian as "terrible." His contract with NBC has prevented him
from an earlier veto of this taping. Menotti refuses
to let NBC show it unless a new production is done.
An NBC executive says the present production cost
around a half million dollars. He points out the
audience rating for AMAHL has gone up since 1963,
although the network was not aiming at the public
mass. Thirteen short paragraphs.

_____. "Swanson's Short Symphony Wins Music Critics
Circle Award Here." January 8, 1952, 23.
Article. NBC Television and Menotti receive a
special citation from the New York Music Critics
Circle for the commission and production of a tele-
vision opera and for the composing. Photo of
Menotti.

_____. Taubman, Howard. "Opera: Yuletide Works."
December 26, 1957, 24.
Review of the NBC Christmas telecast, its seventh
consecutive showing. AMAHL retains its effective
qualities and appeal. Even though opera is not
strongly represented on television, AMAHL gets the
treatment of a "classic." The reason for this is
that its religious aspects have been very influential.
The smooth performance suggests a repertory work.
Kirk Jordan is a "touching" Amahl, Rosemary Kuhlmann the Mother. AMAHL's impact seems to be
growing. Seven paragraphs. Photo of Rosemary
Kuhlmann out of costume.

_____. "Twin Bill in Opera Packs Chautauqua." August
9, 1952, 6.
Article about AMAHL presented by the Chautauqua
Opera Association. The original Amahl, Chet
Allen, attends. His understudy, Richard Mincer,
sings Amahl. Other cast members are listed.

_____. "Two Menotti Operas Given." September 8, 1952,
79.
Brief review of AMAHL at the City Center. Margery
Mayer sings the Mother for the first time. Other
cast members are listed. See also THE OLD
MAID.

_____. "Yonkers Group Gives 'Amahl.'" December 15,
1952, 21.
Brief article about AMAHL in Yonkers, New York.
Baritone Arthur Newman is in the cast. One paragraph.

AMELIA GOES TO THE BALL

_____. Briggs, John. "Records: Operas by Menotti and
Others." December 19, 1954, Section 2:11.
Review of the Angel recording of AMELIA. The
opera remains special. Menotti does not agree that
AMELIA is his best work. The opera is an excellent example of melodic invention and finely developed technical work. The La Scala cast performs
it affectionately. Photo of bass Enrico Campi and
the conductor, Nino Sanzogno. Six paragraphs.

_____. "City Opera Offers Two Menotti Works. " April
25, 1948, 58.
Brief review of AMELIA. Marguerite Piazza
(Amelia), Irwin Dillon (Lover) and Harriet Greene
(Second Maid) are new to their roles. See also
THE OLD MAID.

_____. "The Composer of 'Amelia. ' " February 27,
1938, Section 10:5.
Article. AMELIA was started when Menotti was
22; it is his first opera. His first lessons in orchestration at the Curtis Institute and the writing of
AMELIA coincide. From an early age Menotti was
pulled to the theatre, to Toscanini at La Scala and
other Milan theaters. Menotti says his goals in
writing AMELIA were Falstaff and Le Nozze di
Figaro. Menotti wrote the music and libretto together. AMELIA causes him to receive a commission for radio operas and other offers. Six paragraphs. Photos of Muriel Dickson, Mario Chamlee
and John Brownlee who would sing in the Metropolitan Opera premiere the next Thursday night and
of Menotti.

_____. "Double Bill at Opera. " March 15, 1938, 18.
Brief notice of AMELIA at the Metropolitan Opera
with Ettore Panizza conducting.

_____. Downes, Olin. "Menotti's 'Amelia Goes to the
Ball' Presented at the Metropolitan. " March 4, 1938,
16.
Review of a Metropolitan Opera performance March
3. Downes says the young Menotti has an "instinc-
tive talent. " Menotti shows skill both in drama and
in his vocal writing that is rare in American composers. Even the weakest places are not "affected."
The music is essentially Italian with a strong dis-
play of skill in continuous "musical fabric, " accom-
panied with good characterizations and ensembles
which do not impede the drama. The "slight" story
is used for entertaining stage doings and chatty
music which accompanies the action skillfully. The
work reveals some inexperience for a house as large
as the Metropolitan. The Metropolitan's use of a
stage within a stage works well. Downes praises
the cast but says the orchestration is too "heavy"
for the story and the orchestra too "loud" for the

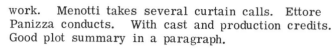

work. Menotti takes several curtain calls. Ettore
Panizza conducts. With cast and production credits.
Good plot summary in a paragraph.

_____. Downes, Olin. "Two Menotti Operas at the City
Center." April 9, 1948, 27.
Review. Although AMELIA greatly amuses, it is
not as "mature" as THE OLD MAID. The cast is
listed; Laszlo Halasz is the conductor. Two paragraphs. See also THE OLD MAID.

_____. "Menotti Opera In Italy." October 9, 1938, Sec-
tion 10:6.
Review of AMELIA AL BALLO at the San Remo
Casino season. It is the season's "hit." Most
music critics of northern and central Italy are more
reserved in their judgment. The production is excellent with sets and costumes by Maria Signorelli.
Luigi Borgonovo is the Husband, Ugo Cantelmo the
Lover and Roberto Silva the Police Chief. Antonino Votto conducts. Three paragraphs.

_____. "Miss O'Malley Sings Menotti Opera Role." Octo-
ber 10, 1948, 68.
Brief notice of the "weaker" AMELIA at the City
Center. Julius Rudel conducts. See also THE OLD
MAID.

_____. Parmenter, Ross. "City Center Gives Two
Menotti Operas." May 6, 1963, 33.
Review of AMELIA at the New York City Opera.
By contrast AMELIA points up the melody in THE
MEDIUM. They are violently opposite works.
AMELIA lacks a strong individual style, but THE
MEDIUM is strangely "Menottian." The cast of
Beverly Bower (Amelia), John Reardon (Husband),
Carl Olson (Lover) and the conductor Felix Popper
is praised. See also THE MEDIUM.

_____. "Schippers Leads Menotti Program." August 1,
1952, 9.
Review of a Lewisohn Stadium concert. On the program is the Overture and an aria from AMELIA.
See also AMAHL and THE ISLAND GOD.

THE CONSUL

_____. May 19, 1950, 30.
Paragraph about THE CONSUL receiving the Sign
Award given by Sign Magazine for the "outstanding
theatrical effort. " Marie Powers and Patricia
Neway are cited for their portrayals.

_____. "Aiken Heard in 'Consul. '" April 17, 1953, 30.
Review of THE CONSUL at the City Center. David
Aiken makes his debut as Mr. Kofner. It is a
"promising one" in this small role. Leon Lishner
takes the Secret Police Agent for the first time with
the New York City Opera. Other cast members
are listed. Four short paragraphs.

_____. "Belgrade Audience Cheers 'The Consul.'" March
17, 1953, 26.
Article about THE CONSUL at the National Theatre
performed by the Belgrade Opera Company. There
are over a dozen curtain calls. The themes have
impact for the audience Its presentation shows the
Communist regime is willing to consider works on
their merits. Milovan Djilas attends. Oskar
Damon is the translator. Five short paragraphs.

_____. "'The Consul. '" January 28, 1951, Section 2:7.
Short article about the many translations of THE
CONSUL for international performances. A box of
two paragraphs.

_____. "'Consul' Cheered in Philadelphia. " March 2,
1950, 32.
Review of THE CONSUL at the Shubert Theatre in
Philadelphia. Marie Powers stops the action with
the Lullaby and Patricia Neway with a later solo.
Both get many cheers. Philadelphia critics acclaim
the "light opera. " Excerpted quote from Menotti on
the people who wait. Composition of the work
started in 1948.

_____. "'Consul' Set in Toronto. " February 12, 1953,
22.
Brief article about the fourth annual Toronto Opera
Festival. Jan Rubes was to sing Mr. Kofner.

_____. Cortesi, Arnaldo. "La Scala Offers Menotti's

'Consul' With Two Members of Original Cast. " January 23, 1951, 24.
   Review of the La Scala premiere. Most of the
   audience gives the opera much applause. Most
   think THE CONSUL should be given at La Scala for
   its bold departure from the usual Italian repertoire.
   Many feel it is more cinematic without distinguished
   music, but they agree it has some excellent episodes. The production is first rate with Menotti as
   the stage director and Nino Sanzogno the conductor.
   Left wing newspapers have been sharply opposed.
   The Corriere della Sera calls the music "old" and
   criticizes it for "depressing" emotion. The Corriere praises Clara Petrella as Magda, Marie
   Powers as the Mother and Andrew McKinley as the
   Conjurer. There are twenty-five curtain calls.
   Principal cast members are listed. Eight paragraphs.

_____. Darlington, W. A. "London Views 'The Mad-
woman of Chaillot' Dimly But Acclaims 'The Consul.'"
March 4, 1951, Section 2:3.
   Notes about the enthusiastic reception of THE CON-
   SUL in London. Two paragraphs.

_____. Downes, Olin. "Menotti: 'Consul' Has Its Pre-
miere. " March 16, 1950, 41.
   Excellent major review of the New York premiere
   at the Barrymore Theatre. It is an overwhelming
   success. Downes gives his highest praise to the
   music, performance, staging and production. The
   cast does wonderfully well in singing Menotti's English text. An orchestral interlude connects the acts.
   Good plot summary in two paragraphs. Downes
   mentions the lullaby and Magda's dream. Menotti
   makes this story tragic, not commonplace. The
   score is very effective--"free rhythms, " effects for
   reality, lyricism. The concerted numbers give
   much contrast for the characters. With precise
   timing Menotti makes the big moment with Magda's
   aria followed by Magda's fainting at the sight of the
   Chief of Police. Patricia Neway's superb Magda
   leads a stellar cast. Marie Powers is a strong
   Mother. Comments on other cast members. Lehman Engel's conducting is praised. The music cannot be considered by itself. Menotti uses a vast
   musical vocabulary effectively. With cast and pro-

duction credits. Fourteen substantial paragraphs.
Photo of Gloria Lane (Secretary) talking on the
phone while Patricia Neway waits.

_____. Downes, Olin. "Opera on Broadway. " April 2,
1950, Section 2:7.
Analytical article on THE CONSUL, its relation to
early opera. Menotti has broken new ground with
a hit opera on Broadway. The Florentines were
originators of opera terminology similar to "musical drama, " "dramma per musica. " The first
operas used a type of recitative, not traditional
melody to convey the text. Melody came as a
second step for emotional intensification and to
sustain song. With instruments accompanying arias,
opera was born. Downes sees weaknesses in THE
CONSUL but states it is a sincere work that belongs
emotionally to its day. THE CONSUL has a "special dramatic character. " Downes quotes Brooks
Atkinson on the indissolubility of THE CONSUL's
music and drama. The ensemble is a device used
to reveal tension and conflict. Menotti uses it with
unusual heat. The lullaby is an example of a set
piece which is not needed dramatically but gives
the role a solo. On the other hand, Magda's aria
is called for by the dramatic situation. Downes
analyzes this aria-scene intelligently. Menotti's
eclecticism--possibly Strauss, much Puccini--is not
uncontrolled. THE CONSUL's achievement is great
next to its weaknesses. Twelve large paragraphs.

_____. Ericson, Raymond. " 'Consul' Offered at State
Theater. " March 18, 1966, 32.
Review of a revival by the New York City Opera.
THE CONSUL retains its power. It is difficult to
assess how much of its staying power is due to
Patricia Neway's Magda. As an opera it has always scored as total theater since neither the music
nor libretto are good enough to make strong musical theater by themselves. The composer's mastery of effects carries the work over its weaker
parts such as the music in general. Neway remains a splendid Magda, although some may feel
she overdoes the role emotionally. Ericson praises
the supporting cast of Sherrill Milnes (Sorel), Herbert Beattie (Secret Police Agent), Beverly Evans
(Secretary), Elizabeth Carron (Foreign Woman) and

the Magician (Gene Bullard). Other members are
listed. Vincent La Selva is the experienced
Menotti conductor. Seven paragraphs.

_____. Gould, Jack. "Triumph on Pay-TV." March 19,
1959, Section 2:13.
Review article of the pay television production
from Toronto. Gould is greatly impressed with the
results. The work is given in its entirety without
interruption. Since Menotti has obvious talents for
this medium, THE CONSUL has an added excitement. The result is a "rare tragic grandeur."
Neway is "unforgettable" in her powerful Magda.
Other cast members praised are Regina Sarfaty
(Secretary), Evelyn Sachs (Mother), Chester Ludgin
(Sorel), Norman Kelley (Magician), Arnold Voketaitis (Mr. Kofner), Maria Marlo (Italian Woman)
and Leon Lishner (Police Agent). The staging is
well adapted for television. Excellent craftsmanship is exhibited in the use of superimposition in
the nightmare scenes. Gould likes the curtain
calls, close-ups for each performer. Sixteen paragraphs.

_____. Gould, Jack. "TV: 'The Consul' for Cash Custo-
mers." March 17, 1959, 61.
Review of a pay television production. Transmission is from Toronto. New York has a private
showing of a tape recording of the Toronto show.
It lasts for two hours, fifteen minutes without any
interruptions. Menotti decided on the intermis-
sions, not the sponsors. Gould rates the production in high terms for television. Its best qualities
are projected well on the small screen. Neway is
just as "unforgettable" on television and her aria,
"To This We've Come" is of classic proportion.
Werner Torkanowsky conducts. John Mason Brown
gives an introduction. Thirteen paragraphs.

_____. Klein, Howard. "City Opera Revives Menotti's
'Consul.'" October 17, 1966, 34.
Review of a revival by the New York City Opera
at Lincoln Center. It may not be a great musical
work, but it shows a great talent theatrically.
Patricia Neway's Magda is supported by David Clatworthy (John Sorel), Julia Migenes (Foreign Woman), La Vergne Monette (Anna Gomez) and Char-

lotte Povia (Vera Boronel).   Charles Wilson conducts.   Three paragraphs.

_____.   "Kuhlmann Scores Hit in 'Consul' at City Center."
October 30, 1952, 41.
Review of Rosemary Kuhlmann's Magda Sorel.   She
wins an ovation at the final curtain for her "moving" interpretation.   She commands all of the role's
facets from the start.   Her "To This We've Come"
is "heartbreaking."   Other leading cast members
are mentioned.   Five paragraphs.

_____.   McLaughlin, Kathleen.   "'Consul' Offered at Fete
in Berlin."   September 8, 1951, 9.
Review of the Berlin premiere at the City Opera
House in the British sector.   The reception is an
enthusiastic one.   Inge Borkh as Magda ignites the
audience.   She receives an ovation of several
minutes after Magda's climactic scene.   Arthur
Rother wins acclaim for his conducting.   Principal
cast members are mentioned.   Eight short paragraphs.

_____.   "Menotti's 'Consul' Opens London Run."   February
8, 1951, 26.
Review of THE CONSUL premiere at the Cambridge
Theater in London.   The opera is again a success.
Menotti is quoted as saying that for the first time,
he wished he had a talent for singing.   THE CON-
SUL will probably outlast THE TELEPHONE and
THE MEDIUM in London.   Patricia Neway wins a
large ovation.   There is more praise from London's
newspaper critics for the singing than for the work.
Excerpts from reviews in The Times and The Daily
Mail, The Daily Telegraph and The News Chronicle.
The Daily Mail critic is excited about Neway's per-
formance.   Ten short paragraphs.

_____.   Parmenter, Ross.   "City Center Gives Opera by
Menotti."   February 15, 1960, 21.
Review of the New York City Opera revival.   The
revival is delayed so Patricia Neway can repeat her
celebrated Magda.   And she makes another great
success in the role.   Her powerful performance
makes the usually climactic appearance of the Police
Chief a tame one.   Also remaining from the last
1953 performance are Horace Armistead's sets.

Werner Torkanowsky conducts. Menotti's forceful
staging makes the new ensemble reminiscent of the
1953 one. Evelyn Sachs makes a strong debut as
the Mother. Newcomers to their roles are given.
Seven paragraphs.

_____. Rich, Alan. "'The Consul' Sung by the City
Opera." March 29, 1962, 28.
Review of a New York City Opera revival. Rich
sees the revival as a "rebuke" to some larger
works done since THE CONSUL's beginning. In its
own context this work is "original," even though
Menotti has definite debts to earlier composers.
Like Hamlet, the opera today has its cliches. A
new director, Roger Englander, does well with an
old production. Werner Torkanowsky conducts well
except when the orchestra drowns out the singers.
Patricia Neway creates "pandemonium" with her
Act II aria. Singing their roles for the first time
are Richard Fredericks (Sorel) Evelyn Sachs
(Mother), William Chapman (Police Agent) and
Marija Kova (Secretary). A less than full house
attends. Eight paragraphs.

_____. Schonberg, Harold C. "'Consul' Is Staged in
Central Park." September 4, 1957, 40.
Review of a production in Central Park's Wolfman
Memorial. The small audience does not augur well
for a run through September. Chandler Cowles
stages with some members of the original cast performing. Amplification gets some competition from
the open air environment plus some amplifier
squeals. It is a simple production. In the cast
are Patricia Neway, Gloria Lane, Maria Marlo,
Lydia Summers (Mother), Norman Atkins (Sorel)
and George Gaynes (Secret Police Agent). Lehman
Engel conducts. Five paragraphs.

_____. Taubman, Howard. "City Opera Adds 'Consul' to
Fare." October 9, 1952, 40.
Review of the New York City Opera's first production. The audience reacts with great enthusiasm.
THE CONSUL is very much of the theatre. Magda's
aria, "To This We've Come" has the necessary in-
gredients to ignite an audience. Patricia Neway
continues to grip one with her Magda. Some parts
are now "pallid" or no longer shock. For the new

listener it should still have great impact.   Gloria
Lane (Secretary), Maria Marlo (Italian Woman),
Vilma Georgiou (Anna Gomez) and Norman Kelley
(Magician) continue to be effective in City Center
debuts.   Some other cast members are mentioned.
Menotti is the stage director, Thomas Schippers
conductor.   Eight paragraphs.

_____.   Taubman, Howard.   "Labeling 'The Consul.' "
March 12 1950, Section 2:1.
Article.   The label "music-drama" may have an
effect on the audience.   Other terms such as "a
play in music" or even "opera" are correct for the
work.   Menotti's subject is the displaced person of
Europe who seeks a new land of freedom.   All
come to the Consul's office for the same reason.
The Consul is never seen.   Menotti's music is
"integral" for his dramatic ideas.   In this work the
drama and music are dependent on each other.
Taubman says the music heightens the drama.   Because of THE MEDIUM and other operas such as
Regina, Broadway is no longer brave in producing
such works.   The producers want eight performances a week.   Cowles and Zimbalist, Jr., have
earmarked $10,000 of the amount raised to carry
the work over possibly weak attendance in the first
weeks.   There is plenty of talent available for other
works like THE CONSUL.   The known member of
the cast is Marie Powers.   Fifteen paragraphs.

_____.   Zolotow, Maurice.   "Patricia Neway Talks of
Magda. "   May 21, 1950, Section 2:1.
Biographical article on Neway that includes material
on the opera.   Neway has taken her critical acclaim in stride.   Neway performs Magda Sorel six
times a week.   Her agent persuaded her to audition for Magda.   Menotti asks her for three auditions.   During rehearsals she had recurring doubts
about her ability to handle the role.   She uses a
personal experience of being hit by a car and the
subsequent "red tape" to build Magda's frustration
and anger.   Photo of Neway as Magda.

THE DEATH OF THE BISHOP OF BRINDISI

_____.   Parmenter, Ross.   "Music: Menotti Cantata. "

May 20, 1963, 36.
Review of the world premiere performance at the
Cincinnati May Festival. The Music Hall is filled
to capacity. An audience of many parents takes
pride in the work. The children are excellent
singers and the cantata an enormous success. They
cheer Menotti. Menotti's storm music has the
same skill he brought to the subway music of THE
SAINT. The music for the frightened children
makes an emotional impact. Parmenter compares
the Bishop's guilt to Madame Flora's in THE MED-
IUM and the tension in THE CONSUL's first act.
Parmenter believes the denouement is not wholly
satisfying for the work's questions. Richard Cross
sings the Bishop and Rosalind Elias the Nun. The
townspeople are sung by the May Festival Chorus
and the University of Kentucky Northern Center
Chorus. Twelve paragraphs.

_____. Schonberg, Harold C. "Music: New Choral Work
by Menotti." October 22, 1964, 42.
Review of the first New York performance in Phil-
harmonic Hall performed by the Boston Symphony.
Menotti and Britten are much taken with the purity
of young voices. The Menotti text, reminiscent of
Robert Browning, has the Bishop asking "eternal"
questions about his beliefs. Schonberg calls it
"good background music" and the score "bland."
George London and Lili Chookasian are the soloists.
Choral work is performed by several choral groups.
Photo of Erich Leinsdorf and Menotti looking at the
score. Five paragraphs.

HELP! HELP! THE GLOBOLINKS ARE COMING

_____. Henahan, Donal. "Amahl and 'Globolinks' Per-
formed." December 24, 1970, 10.
Review of HELP! at the ANTA Theater. June
Cooper is the effective Emily. Other cast members are mentioned. One paragraph.

_____. "Opera Has American Premiere." August 3,
1969, 66.
Photo of the invading space people from the Santa
Fe production.

_____. Schonberg, Harold C. "Did Menotti Beat 'The Devils'?" August 24, 1969, Section 2:5.
Article contrasting the Menotti career including HELP! with Penderecki and his opera. The Devils of Loudun. Schonberg sees the new Menotti as a "conscious attack" on Penderecki's type of music. Menotti grew up as a new "romantic" in the 1930s and 1940s. Schonberg claims the critics of those decades were not sympathetic to atonal composers such as Webern and Berg and welcomed Menotti's operas. After World War II a new generation of critics, closer to the atonal composer, saw Menotti as "old fashioned" or "naive" while the public continued to like his operas. Menotti refused to join the trend toward serialism and Schonberg points to the relatively weak MARIA and THE LAST SAVAGE as examples of his persistent opposition to serial music. In HELP! Menotti takes on the critics by saying the work is not for them and then using "polemics in disguise" in the opera, for the opera's message is that music written for the heart will redeem mankind, not the electronic music of the Globolinks, representatives of composers of serial and abstract music. Schonberg praises the new opera, to him a "musical comedy" more than an opera, for its staging, choreography and its "charm." The audiences loved it at Santa Fe. Five large paragraphs.

_____. Schonberg, Harold C. "Menotti's Globolinks Invade Santa Fe." August 18 1969, 28.
Review of the Santa Fe Opera production. In his attack on abstract music, Menotti proclaims this opera is for children since they are the only "candid" audience left. To Schonberg Menotti presents an obvious parable. He is saying that only music of feeling and emotion can save the world. The Globolinks symbolize a mechanized world. Menotti continues his "neo-Puccini" style of music although it is superior to some of his recent music and has some charm. The audience gives generous approval. There is much fun in watching the Globolinks, their costumes and movements. This fourth performance at Santa Fe is overseen by Menotti and has a good cast. Marguerite Willauer as Madame Euterpova and Judith Blegen as the violin-playing Emily are the big successes. Ten para-

graphs.   Photos of the Globolinks "skimming" in
the Santa Fe production and of Menotti.

_____.   Schonberg, Harold.   "Opera: Two By Menotti. "
December 23, 1969, 21.
Review of HELP! at the City Center.   This new
opera makes a good impression.   One can hear this
as a story or as Menotti's music which Schonberg
implies always is the same.   Schonberg finds it
difficult to be serious toward Menotti's idiom.   It is
possible to take the opera as an allegory aimed
against modern or electronic music.   Madame Euterpova expresses this attack on electronic music.
And there is electronic music which is not very
atonal in the score.   Schonberg likes Alwin Nikolais' Globolinks better than anything.   On the other
hand the audience is enthusiastic about the total
affair.   Judith Blegen sings Emily and plays the
violin.   Schonberg compliments the rest of the cast
also.   Eight paragraphs.   Photo of Judith Blegen
(Emily) and Ellen Faull (Mme. Euterpova).   See
also AMAHL.

_____.   Sutcliffe, James H.   "Help! The Globolinks Are
Coming. "   December 29, 1968, Section 2: 15.
Article.   Menotti pokes fun at a math teacher, a
literature expert and a biologist in his new opera.
The first audience in Hamburg shows great enjoy-
ment.   Most of the fun, however, comes from
Madame Euterpova, a music teacher of the old
school.   Arlene Saunders wins an ovation at Hamburg for this role.   HELP! is in one act with four
scenes running an hour and ten minutes.   Compared
to AMAHL, Sutcliffe thinks it is not as dramatically
cohesive.   He points to passages which recall
Madame Butterfly, MARIA GOLOVIN and his Violin
Concerto.   Menotti surprises one with his use of
electronic music, partly tonal.   Choreographer
Alwin Nikolais has designed imaginative Globolink
costumes, "seven-foot high stacks of white elastic
top hats. "   The unusual lighting is by Nicolas
Schoeffer.   In the course of the story are a tuba
solo, Madame Euterpova's pedagogy on orchestral
instruments, a "canonic lament" and other puns.
Menotti's message is that only music addressed to
the emotions or heart will save humanity from a
super machine age.   Some of the avantgarde in

Hamburg boo. Ten large paragraphs. Photo of
Menotti.

THE ISLAND GOD

_____. March 8, 1942, Section 8:7.
Photo of a setting of the opera with Telea and two
of the male characters shown.

_____. Downes, Olin. " 'Island God' Opera Heard in
Premiere. " February 21, 1942, 14.
Important review of the world premiere performance
at the Metropolitan Opera. Downes points out it is
Menotti's first effort in serious opera. The "melodic gift" is lacking in THE ISLAND GOD. The
fault is with the undramatic story, with a love situation not realized. Menotti cannot make these
characters live. There is no "dramatic development" as the story unfolds. Occasionally Menotti
is lyrical with the duet being the climax musically.
Downes quotes phrases from the duet, "The Ocean.
The Silence. " He tells why he considers this duet
reminiscent of Puccini. The other solo vocal passages, such as one for Telea, are not convincing
music. The cast makes the most of the roles. The
cast is Ilo (Leonard Warren), Telea (Astrid Varnay), Luca (Raoul Jobin), a Greek God (Norman
Gordon) and Voice of a Fisherman (John Carter).
The conductor is Ettore Panizza, the stage director
Lothar Wallerstein in a Fleming Macliesh version.
Plot summary in four short paragraphs. Over one
column.

_____. '"The Island God' Heard. " March 3, 1942, 27.
Review of the second performance at the Met. The
work receives a "cordial reception. " Two short
paragraphs.

_____. "Schippers Leads Menotti Program. " August 1,
1952, 9.
Review of a Lewisohn Stadium concert. Soprano
Eileen Farrell and tenor Wesley Dalton sing the
duet from THE ISLAND GOD. See also AMAHL and
AMELIA.

_____. "Two Operas Presented. " March 13, 1942, 16.

Brief notice of the final performance at the Metropolitan Opera with cast listing and conductor.

THE LAST SAVAGE

_____. January 28, 1964, 24.
A Metropolitan Opera ad to promote THE LAST
SAVAGE over Harold Schonberg's negative review.
There are excerpts from reviews in the Herald
Tribune, Daily News, Journal American, World
Telegram and Post, all praising the new comic
opera.   The ad asks, "Which Paper Do You Read?"

_____. Lenoir, Jean-Pierre. "Opera by Menotti Offered
in Paris."   October 23, 1963, 37.
Article about the world premiere performance at
the Opera-Comique in Paris October 22.   It was
commissioned by a Paris Opera administrator.
Menotti satirizes abstract artists, poets, beatniks,
and so forth.   Much of the opera is not Menotti's
best work.   Weakest is the first scene.   Mady
Mesple (Kitty) and Adriana Maliponte (Sardula) are
called the best in the cast.   Andre Beaurepaire's
sets are best for the American scenes. Brief plot
summary.

_____. Menotti, Gian-Carlo.   "The 'Last Savage' Arrives
at the Met." January 19, 1964, Section 2:13.
Menotti discusses his comic opera at the Metropolitan Opera.   He says laughter in comic opera
comes from the music.   The audience does not
need to laugh if the music does.   The French
critics lash Menotti for his playful poke at dodec-
aphonic music.   In this opera the laughing is
gentle and ironic.   In THE LAST SAVAGE he seeks
to restore grace and sweetness rather than pro-
moting a more "fashionable jargon."   Photo of the
Met production with a caged George London (title
role) in the Maharajah's palace with Ezio Flagello,
Teresa Stratas, Nicolai Gedda, Lili Chookasian,
Morley Meredith and Roberta Peters.

_____. "New Menotti Opera Interests the Met." January
24, 1959, 13.
Article.   Dr. Franco Colombo says the Paris
Opera Commission of THE LAST SAVAGE is the

first to a non-French composer in over a century.
Five paragraphs.

_____. Parmenter, Ross. "Music World: Superman Put
Off. " March 11, 1962, Section 2:11.
Article. For the third time The Last Superman
has been postponed. The problem is in getting a
French translation of the Italian libretto that meets
Menotti's approval. There is not enough time for
an attempt of a third translation. And it is decided the opera is too small for the size of the
Paris Opera. THE MEDIUM is given by the Opera-
Comique without Menotti's staging; he tells his dislike of the staging to the French press. He is
pleased that the Comique will do the opera since he
has more time for polishing it. He will stage the
Metropolitan Opera's first performance in January,
1964. Six paragraphs.

_____. Schonberg, Harold. "Opera: 'The Last Savage.'"
January 24, 1964, 20.
Review of the United States debut at the Metropolitan Opera. The opening night audience finds much
amusing. Some of the humor points back at the
composer since his satire of electrododecaphonic
music reminds the critic that Menotti is not skillful at composing dissonant music. The music is
not "good. " It is a mixture of Gilbert and Sullivan,
Richard Rodgers, Rossini, Donizetti, Wagner--
nineteenth century musical writing for a modern
theme. To Schonberg it is more of a Broadway
musical in which Menotti has to rely on situation
for comedy because the music does not make the
comic spirit. The libretto is weak, on the level
of a television serial. Best is the production and
Beni Montresor's sets. Teresa Stratas (Sardula)
wins special praise. Other good performances
come from Ezio Flagello, Morley Meredith and Lili
Chookasian. George London is ideal in the title
role, physically suited and musically intelligent.
Nicolai Gedda and Roberta Peters are less comfort-
able in their singing roles. Thomas Schippers
conducts. With cast and production credits. Ten
paragraphs. Photo of the caged Savage (George
London) and Teresa Stratas, Ezio Flagello, Lili
Chookasian, Roberta Peters, Morley Meredith and
Nicolai Gedda. Ten paragraphs.

_____. Strongin, Theodore. "'The Last Savage' Is
Given at Met. " January 1, 1965, 11.
     Review of a Met New Year's Eve performance.
     Rudolph Bing and Leontyne Price come on stage
     during the cocktail party scene. Robert La March-
     ina makes his Met conducting debut. It is a "stiff"
     performance of the ordinary music. Leading sing-
     ers perform well. Teresa Stratas and John Alex-
     ander are singled out for praise. Robert Nagy and
     Calvin Marsh take smaller roles for the first time.
     Nine short paragraphs.

MARIA GOLOVIN

_____. November 2, 1958, Section 2:1.
     Photo with Franca Duval (Maria) and Richard Cross
     (Donato) in the New York production.

_____. Atkinson, Brooks. "Theatre: 'Maria Golovin. ' "
November 6, 1958, 43.
     Review of MARIA at the Martin Beck Theatre. This
     is "prosaic" compared to THE SAINT. Although it
     is his "least original" opera, it still exhibits a
     high talent. The theme is small compared to
     earlier works such as THE CONSUL and THE
     SAINT. Menotti has done everything but design
     and sing the parts. Atkinson points out Menotti's
     traditional musical position and notes the "lampoon"
     of modernism in the third act. Menotti is able to
     give even minor passages a lovely feel. Rather
     than overpowering the audience, Menotti and the
     singers go at their jobs with ease. Franca Duval
     and Richard Cross are excellent as Maria and
     Donato. Atkinson mentions also the work of Pa-
     tricia Neway (Mother), Ruth Kobart (Agata), Nor-
     man Kelley (Dr. Zuckertanz) and William Chapman
     (Prisoner). Although this is not major Menotti,
     Atkinson praises Menotti's talent and the discipline
     of the singers. Brief story sketch. With cast and
     production credits. Photo of Franca Duval and
     Richard Cross. Nine paragraphs.

_____. Gelb, Arthur. "Theatrical Suspense in a Com-
poser's World. " November 2, 1958, Section 2:1, 3.
     Gelb talks to Menotti about MARIA and his work in
     general. Menotti says that MARIA returns to THE

MEDIUM's style and departs from the tradition of
THE CONSUL. Drama takes precedence. Menotti
cannot pinpoint how ideas come to him. His
maimed heroes may be a symbol of himself. His
composing is slowly done. He needs good singers,
a suitable theater and freedom; he wants to make
demands and get them realized. Photo of Franca
Duval and Richard Cross.

_____. "Menotti: At Work on a New Opera. " February
18, 1958, 24.
Article largely about Menotti's writing of MARIA
GOLOVIN for the International Exposition in Brus-
sels. NBC has commissioned the new work. Listed
are the to-be producer, conductor and designer.
Menotti describes it as a "romantic tragedy. "
Menotti sums up the "psychological content. " The
cast will be eight plus an off-stage chorus of eight.
Ten paragraphs.

_____. Mintz, Donald. "Opera by Menotti Has Second
Premiere. " January 25, 1965, 22.
Review of the revised MARIA performed by the
Opera Society of Washington, D. C. Menotti's state-
ment on the revision is quoted. He has made
"minute" changes and much re-orchestrating. Although audience reaction is good, Mintz says the
work is still a problem. He says the libretto is
the problem. This is "sleazy" melodrama with weak
symbolism. The commonplace text does not aid the
music. The women's trio and the Act III love duet
are praised. Some have called the style "Holly-
woodized Puccini. " Cast and production are excellent. Thirteen short paragraphs.

_____. Taubman, Howard. "Don't Say Opera: Broadway
Producers Will Do Anything to Disguise the Terrible
Truth. " November 30, 1958, Section 2:11.
MARIA and opera on Broadway. Broadway producers want to disguise opera and call it something
else. MARIA demonstrates the schizophrenic nature
of Broadway. The producers seem to categorize
the public as one ignorant of Menotti's past triumphs. MARIA's run is quite short. It is of higher quality than some of Broadway's shows. The
scene in the second act for the three women illustrates how only opera can use several voices at once.

MARIA is too good to be called a failure.

_____. Taubman, Howard. "Opera: 'Maria Golovin.'"
March 9, 1959, 35.
Review of the NBC Opera Company production. NBC
has been a giant in the early history of this opera.
It lasted only a few nights on Broadway. It comes
across with power on television. The veteran cast
integrates acting with singing well. All of the cast
is excellent as singing actors. Taubman reasserts
that MARIA is better than its Broadway experience
suggests although it has weak points. Both visually
and aurally the production is impressive. Cast and
production credits. Ten paragraphs. Photo of
Franca Duval.

_____. Taubman, Howard. "Opera: Menotti Premiere in
Brussels." August 21, 1958, 23.
Review of the Brussels premiere. MARIA is typi-
cally Menotti in its theatricality. NBC made the
opera possible and sent its company to do the Brussels production. MARIA's strength is its libretto
which has appeal to the sentimental. The characters are sympathetically drawn. Menotti is very
concerned with dramatic effect, as with the second
act close. This music does not impede the story's
progress. One theme is illustrated in the second
act trio, that of contrasting past happiness with
present misfortune. There are instances for the
music to add a colorful voice. But the main impression is of music serving the libretto in a
secondary role. Stylistically this is more Italian
romantic music. Menotti takes a poke at modernism through the role of the tutor. The production
realizes the opera's range well. Richard Cross,
the young blind man, is a "find." Other cast members are also admired. Sixteen paragraphs. Photo
of Franca Duval (Maria).

_____. Taubman, Howard. "Opera: Series Made in
America." March 31, 1959, 24.
Review of the New York City Opera premiere. This
new production is another chance for MARIA to
prove itself again after its flop on Broadway.
Menotti's revisions give it a tightened orchestral
role. MARIA makes for effective theatre. The
characters are mixed in their dramatic worth.

While it is realized well, the prisoner is not "vital" and the tutor is irrelevant. The best parts are when Menotti lets his lyrical expression out. Taubman reasserts that while it is not Menotti's best, it deserves a public. The City Center gives an excellent account. The cast is praised as are the director, Kirk Browning, conductor Herbert Grossman, designer Rouben Ter-Arutunian and costumer Ruth Morley. Cast and production credits boxed. Ten paragraphs. Photos of Richard Cross (Donato) and Ilona Kombrink (Maria) in the City Center production.

_____. Taubman, Howard. "Operatic Fusion: Drama, Music Joined Skillfully by Menotti." August 31, 1958, 7.

Analysis of MARIA in relation to the total Menotti. MARIA combines his merits and demerits. Menotti knows how to write a concise libretto, but they do not point to a career in spoken drama. MARIA's denouement would be less effective in drama. The style is very romantic. Dr. Zuckertanz illustrates the avant-garde; his character is a digression. The music is nostalgic and the score not "distinguished," for it does not make one identify with the characters. Taubman asserts that superior opera captures the emotions of its characters, but Menotti's operas often do not achieve this important level. Menotti's ability to write a libretto and music that need to go together produces "workmanlike" theatre. He is beyond comparison in using the varied "resources of the lyric theatre." Photos: The full MARIA cast, Menotti and conductor Peter Herman Adler in rehearsal at Spoleto and a scene from MARIA with Richard Cross, Patricia Neway and Franca Duval.

MARTIN'S LIE

_____. Baro, Gene. "A Boy Befriends a Heretic." June 14, 1964, Section 2:11.

Review of the world premiere in Bristol Cathedral at the Bath Festival in England. Bristol Cathedral presents big acoustical problems. Its mixed reviews in the British press probably indicate it needs to be heard in a more intimate setting. Two para-

graphs sketch the plot. His serious theme deserves
attention. Baro says the composer has handled the
musical exposition well with such "lean" material.
The cast is very good. Photo of Michael Wennink
(Martin) and Donald McIntyre (Heretic).

_____. Baro, Gene. "Opera by Menotti Bows in Eng-
land." June 5, 1964, 25.
Review of the world premiere at the Bath Festival
June 3. It is a dramatic work of less than an
hour. We are confronted with abstractions. Menotti
keeps us in contact with emotion continually. This
is "simplified seriousness" which will be adaptable
for amateur groups. MARTIN'S LIE is on such a
small scale that it should benefit from television,
but it is out of place in a cathedral. Michael Wennink as Martin is an effective boy actor. Plot
summary.

_____. Klein, Howard. "TV: New Menotti Opera." May
31, 1965, 31.
Review of a CBS television production, the United
States premiere. An earlier scheduled telecast was
cancelled for a tribute to Sir Winston Churchill.
Klein calls the short opera absorbing up to Martin's death. Menotti is on screen as a narrator.
The conclusion to Klein is that of a "musical tear-
jerker," too facilely handled. A medieval style is
used. The semimelodic recitative adds an excess
of color and slows the rate of speech. Klein concludes that the music is not as strong as the story.
Good plot summary. Twelve paragraphs.

THE MEDIUM

_____. Atkinson, Brooks. "'Medium' Revisited."
September 3, 1950, Section 2:1.
Review of THE MEDIUM at the Arena in the Hotel
Edison. Zelma George is the effective Madame
Flora. She overwhelms the story with her large
portrayal even though she is not as accomplished a
singer as Marie Powers. The rest of the company
is also excellent. The Arena is more intimate
making the dialogue more intelligible while the
Armistead sets have been sacrificed. The performance is a great success and may indicate a

long run at the Arena.

_____. "Ann Ayars Is Monica in Opera by Menotti. "
November 7, 1949, 32.
Review at the City Center. Ann Ayars is a good
actress and her voice is well produced. Two
paragraphs. See also THE OLD MAID.

_____. Briggs, John. "Opera: Two By Menotti. " April
21, 1958, 20.
Review at the City Center. Evan Whallon debuts as
conductor and Joan Carroll as Monica. Her singing is sometimes "unsteady. " Another debut is
Marc Scott as Toby. Claramae Turner is the Mme.
Flora; other singers are mentioned. Five paragraphs. See also THE OLD MAID.

_____. "Brooklyn Hears Two by Menotti. " December 14,
1955, 52.
Brief review of THE MEDIUM at the Brooklyn
Academy of Music. Marie Powers is Mme. Flora.
Since the writer feels the second act is weaker
than the strong first, he calls it an "uneven" work,
close to greatness. Other cast members are given.
Emanuel Balaban conducts. See also THE TELE-
PHONE.

_____. "City Opera Closes Its 'Best' Season. " May 2,
1949, 20.
Notes on THE MEDIUM in a summary of the New
York City Opera spring season. Dorothy MacNeil
is a hit as Monica in the final weekend. See also
THE OLD MAID.

_____. "City Opera Stages Menotti Twin Bill. " March
23, 1953, 27.
Review at the City Center. Claramae Turner makes
her New York City Opera debut as Madame Flora.
She is cheered for her performance. Chet Allen,
the first Amahl, plays his first Toby successfully.
Virginia Haskins is also a new Monica. Four paragraphs. See also AMAHL.

_____. Crowther, Bosley. "The Screen: Three Films in
Local Premieres. " September 6, 1951, 39.
Review of THE MEDIUM film premiere at the
Salton Theatre. It still has melodramatic punch in

a different medium. Pictorially the wide use of
the camera makes it "charged. " But there is some
"inconsistency. " Some scenes work better than
others. Even in the slower sequences, there is
"graphic power. " It is valid as drama for the
screen. A typical film audience may find the recitative "disconcerting. " Although Alberghetti sings
well, she seems awkward in communicating while
singing. Leo Coleman as the mute embarrasses
one with his show. To Crowther this filmed opera
is "thin. " Photo of Marie Powers as Mme. Flora.

_____. "Double Bill Is Sung. " April 28, 1958, 27.
Brief notice of a performance at the City Center.
See also THE OLD MAID.

_____. Downes, Edward. "Patricia Neway Sings Opera
Role. " May 2, 1958, 31.
Review at the City Center. Patricia Neway sings
Mme. Flora for the first time. Neway does pro-
ject a strong interpretation, but Downes feels she
needs to lower the intensity of her performance at
the start. By the time she reaches her solo scene,
"Afraid? " she has to shout and exaggerate the hor-
ror in a manner that could be improved. Also new
to their roles are Lee Venora (Monica) and Helen
Baisley (Mrs. Nolan). Five paragraphs. See also
THE OLD MAID.

_____. Downes, Olin. "Marie Powers Hit in Menotti
Operas. " April 8, 1949, 31.
Review at the City Center. Downes believes the
pairing of THE MEDIUM and THE OLD MAID
makes for top entertainment. Marie Powers is a
great success in the title role. She does not have
to rely on acting to make up for a weak voice. It
benefits from a large stage for more perspective
and a larger orchestra. The performers have ma-
tured in their parts and the audience cheers. See
also THE OLD MAID.

_____. Downes, Olin. "Menotti: Pioneer. His Movie
Adaptation of 'The Medium' Heralds Way Toward
Screen Opera. " September 16, 1951, Section 2:9.
Major consideration of the screen premiere of THE
MEDIUM. Downes feels the screen version is only
partly effective. Some reasons for this are tech-

nical. The synchronizing is crude. There are in-
sufficient resources for the pictorial aspects.
THE CONSUL may be more appropriate for screen
when one thinks of material such as the dream
dance episode. One method of opera production for
movies and television is simply the filming of an
actual performance. The other is a new presentation not yet seen. Since Menotti is both composer and librettist he may become the leading composer for screen opera. In the new form vocalism
would need to be superseded by sight and sound.
Wagner's operas hint at this procedure. Menotti
may be just the composer for an original opera for
screen.

_____. Downes, Olin. "Opera by Menotti Has Its Pre-
miere." February 19, 1947, 32.
Review of the revised opera at the Heckscher The-
atre. Menottis has given more "concentration" to
the first act. The first act lacks the more dra-
matic material of the second. Regardless of whom
Menotti has been influenced by, this is strong
opera. Downes gives a paragraph in praise of
Marie Power's singing and acting, a "great actress."
He calls Leo Coleman's mute "unforgettable."
Other cast members are mentioned as is conductor
Leon Barzin. Four paragraphs. See also THE
TELEPHONE.

_____. "It Happens in Music." May 5, 1946, Section
2:5.
Article about the upcoming world premiere of THE
MEDIUM at Columbia University's Brander Matthews Theatre. Menotti calls it a work in the
"grand guignol" school. A quote from his program
notes about the two worlds of the work. The scoring is given. An unusual aspect is a love duet for
one character. Menotti is "enthusiastic" about the
cast and conductor.

_____. "Menotti, Gian-Carlo. "Trials and Tribulations
of 'The Medium.'" August 26, 1951, Section 2:5.
Article by the composer on the experiences of the
film. When Menotti asks for the "impossible," he
gets such through Sasha Hammid and Enzo Serafin,
both cameramen. He misses the stage's "spontaneity." The script is thrown out as improvisa-

tion becomes the order. He has to work with a
pre-recorded soundtrack making some "good shots"
bad because of synchronization problems. Certainly
he does not "enjoy" the filming.

_____. Mitgang, Herbert. "Being a Tale of Film-Making
in Three Cities. " June 24 1951, Section 2:5.
Article in part about the film production of THE
MEDIUM. According to the film's producer, Walter
Lowendahl, Menotti fought against tradition in the
filming. For instance, he asked for unusually close
close-ups.

_____. Parmenter, Ross. "City Center Gives Two
Menotti Operas. " May 6, 1963, 33.
Review at the New York City Opera. THE MED
MEDIUM is more of a success than AMELIA. Con-
ductor Robert LaMarchina has much to do with its
dramatic impact. Lili Chookasian scores a triumph
as Madame Flora with an excellent natural voice.
Other cast members win Parmenter's praise.
Menotti, who stages both operas, joins in the last
curtain calls. See also AMELIA.

_____. Shanley, J. P. "By Popular Demand. " January
2, 1949, Section 2:3.
Article about the success of THE MEDIUM and
THE TELEPHONE in the United States and abroad.
The double bill was threatened with being closed
nineteen months ago at the Barrymore Theatre.
There were two handicaps as theatre, opera and
the lack of stars in the casts. Chandler Cowles
decided to keep the run longer which led to greater
public interest. The two play until November 2,
1947, with no week being a loss. A recent New
York revival is extended. Many other international
productions are possible. In Paris the casts have
less than five days to learn their roles in French.
The costumes and sets arrive late. Because of
language problems, Cowles, Menotti and David Kantor hang the sets. There is no orchestra pit.
Without a dress rehearsal the performances of both
are acclaimed by French writers. Excerpt from
the review in Paris-Presse (generous praise). No
profit is made in Paris due to the technical problems. Sixteen paragraphs. See also THE TELE-
PHONE.

_____. Taubman, Howard. "The Opera: City Center
Double Bill. " April 17, 1959, 21.
Brief review of THE MEDIUM at the City Center.
Taubman underlines THE MEDIUM's importance.
Newcomers to the opera with the New York City
Opera are Joy Clements (Monica), Jose Perez
(Toby) and Werner Torkanowsky, conductor, in his
debut. With cast and production credits.

_____. Taubman, Howard. "Opera on the Loose. "
October 2, 1949, Section 2:7.
Article. Taubman asserts THE MEDIUM is an
opera in every way. Euphemisms for it are there
since it is given on Broadway. THE MEDIUM has
been performed six hundred times on Broadway, on
television and elsewhere. For an opera this is an
enormous feat. First THE MEDIUM gets a few
performances at Columbia University and at the
Heckscher Theatre. On Broadway it is disguised
as a "music drama" for seven months before tour-
ing. With Marie Powers it goes to London for a
month. Some English rate Menotti below Britten.
In Paris it is praised although the French parts are
learned very quickly. It is now being performed
by amateur groups, summer theatres, a Negro cast
in Cleveland and is invited abroad. Authorities in
Germany have banned it for reasons of depressing
Germans which is hard to accept. New Orleans
had plans to produce it, but a Negro mute brought
objections. Menotti has received many film offers.
His new work, THE CONSUL, will pattern THE
MEDIUM in the use of recitative modeled after
Monteverdi's declamation.

_____. "Two Menotti Operas Heard. " October 17, 1949,
19.
Brief notice of THE MEDIUM at the City Center.
The cast is Marie Powers, Dorothy MacNeil, Leo
Coleman, Leona Scheuremann, Edwin Dunning and
Frances Bible with Joseph Rosenstock as conductor.
See also THE OLD MAID.

_____. "Two Menotti Operas in Unusual Show. " July 20,
1950, 22.
Review of THE MEDIUM at the Arena. Perhaps
this is the first time in New York City for opera
"in the round. " The reviewer has doubts about

using two pianos for accompaniment. THE MED-
IUM comes across best. Zelma George wins cheers
for her Madame Flora though her characterization
seems "forced" near the end. The rest of the cast
is excellent. Photo of Zelma George as Madame
Flora. See also THE TELEPHONE.

_____. Weiler, A. H. "Random Notes on the Music
Scene." March 26, 1950, Section 2:5.
Article about Menotti's experiences with Hollywood.
Hollywood is making offers to film THE MEDIUM.
The composer doubts if it will be filmed there. He
underlines the difficulty of going into different
mediums with the same work. In his earlier ex-
perience with Hollywood he wrote two scripts which
were rejected. THE MEDIUM will be filmed in
Rome with Menotti directing.

THE MOST IMPORTANT MAN

Christian Science Monitor (Midwest Edition). Kastendieck,
Miles. "A Menotti Premiere...." March 22, 1971,
5.
Review of the New York City Opera world premiere
production. All is superb except the opera. There
is a weak libretto, a weak final act and an uncon-
vincing love interest. The story does not seem
tragic. The "lovely melodies" do not make a
strong dramatic situation. The production team of
Menotti (stage director), Oliver Smith (designer)
and Christopher Keene (conductor) is skillful.
Eugene Holmes, Joanna Bruno, Beverly Wolff and
Harry Theyard are the impressive lead singers.
Six paragraphs.

New York Times. Schonberg, Harold. "The Opera: Menotti's
'Important Man.'" March 14, 1971, 6.
Review of the New York City Opera production
March 12. Schonberg says most of it "is more
soap opera" than good music. Some things are
funny although not intended. Puccini's influence is
heavy. The most unusual music is the use of
African sounding rhythms. The work fails as a
total conception. The production is praised as is
the "superior" cast. In one scene Menotti uses the
ideas of Kurt Jooss' ballet, The Green Table. But

there are too many cliches. Plot summary.

THE OLD MAID AND THE THIEF

_____. "Ann Ayars Is Monica in Opera by Menotti. "
November 7, 1949, 32.
Brief notice at the City Center. Adelaide Bishop
is the Old Maid, John Tyers Bob. See also THE
MEDIUM.

_____. "Behind the Scenes. " March 19, 1939, Section
11:12.
Article announcing the world premiere of THE OLD
MAID on radio.

_____. Briggs, John. "Opera: Two By Menotti. " April
21, 1958, 20.
Review of a City Center performance. Briggs
calls the performance a "gem. " The principals
make the audience enthusiastic. Two short paragraphs. See also THE MEDIUM.

_____. "City Opera Closes Its 'Best' Season. " May 2,
1949, 20.
Notes on THE OLD MAID in a summary of the
New York City Opera spring season. See also
THE MEDIUM.

_____. "City Opera Offers Menotti Program. " Septem-
ber 20, 1952, 12.
Review of a performance at the City Center. Some
of the humor has not lasted. Cast members are
mentioned. Thomas Schippers conducts. See also
AMAHL.

_____. "City Opera Offers Two Menotti Works. " April
25, 1948, 58.
Brief review. Baritone Andrew Gainey makes his
City Center debut as Bob. His portrayal is effective. Mary Kreste sings Miss Todd to the audience's pleasure. Thomas P. Martin conducts. See
also AMELIA.

_____. "Double Bill Is Sung. " April 28, 1958, 27.
Review. Lee Venora sings Laetitia for the first
time successfully at the City Center. Other cast

members are listed. Three short paragraphs.
See also THE MEDIUM.

_____. Downes, Edward. "Patricia Neway Sings Opera
Role. " May 2, 1958, 31.
Review of THE OLD MAID at the City Center. New
to their roles are Beatrice Krebs (Miss Todd),
Elizabeth Carson (Miss Pinkerton) and William
Metcalf (Bob). Although they sing well, clearer
diction and more dash in acting are needed. Two
paragraphs. See also THE MEDIUM.

_____. Downes, Olin. "City Opera Offers Menotti's
'Amahl.'" April 10, 1952, 36.
Short notice at the City Center with AMAHL. This
amusing work lacks the maturity and significance
of AMAHL. See also AMAHL.

_____. Downes, Olin. "Marie Powers Hit in Menotti
Operas. " April 8, 1949, 31.
Review at the City Center. Marie Powers brings
distinction with skilled farce to Miss Todd. Others
in the cast are Virginia MacWatters (Laetitia),
Ellen Faull (Miss Pinkerton), and Norman Young
(Bob). An enthusiastic capacity audience attends.
See also THE MEDIUM.

_____. Downes, Olin. "Two Menotti Operas at the City
Center. " April 9, 1948, 27.
Review at the City Center. Downes sees THE
OLD MAID as successful enough to endure in the
repertory. It astonishes one familiar with the
radio opera. The audience laughs heartily at the
humor. To Downes it is a triumph of "natural-
ness, " an opera buffa that is Menotti's best work
yet. The performance gets Downes' admiration,
also. Plot summary in a paragraph. Marie
Powers (Old Maid), Virginia MacWatters (Servant),
Ellen Faull (Miss Pinkerton) and Norman Young
(Bob) are all right for their roles. Six paragraphs.
See also AMELIA.

_____. Dunlap, Orrin E., Jr. "Radio 'Capsule' Opera
Ready for a Spring Premiere. " April 16, 1939,
Section 10:12.
Article about the forthcoming broadcast and the
problems of opera on radio. Menotti was com-

missioned over a year ago by NBC to make an
opera for radio. Menotti, according to Dunlap,
looked at the commission in a practical way, an
opportunity for cash. Menotti thinks an opera
written for radio might be transferred to the screen
more readily than the usual staged opera. The
radio opera's brevity is simply a composing reality.
The key idea is simplicity in the radio production.
Menotti says radio has the advantage of allowing
the composer to reach young singers eager for experience. Words for a staged opera and a radio
one may be different of necessity. As an example,
Menotti had to fight to retain THE OLD MAID AND
THE THIEF as a title for radio. Menotti said he
would compose an opera, "The Sleeping Man," if a
new commission came. Singers will be Mary
Hopple, Robert Weede, Margaret Daum and Willa
Stewart. Slightly over a column. Photos of Mary
Hopple (Old Maid), Robert Weede (Bob) and Menotti
at twenty-eight.

_____. Dunlap, Orrin E., Jr. "Radio Opera Reveals
the Need of Melody to Enchant the Unseen Audience."
April 30, 1939, Section 11:12.
Article about the premiere performance and the reaction of music critics and radio circles. Listeners at home think it is too conversational and lacks
"sustained melody." Both critics and listeners
agree on the conductor's and soloists' excellence.
One official thinks it is a possiblity for television
production. Technically and electrically it is a
"radio masterpiece." It could have been more of
an entertainment to the radio audience. For them
it is the enduring melody that is important. Six
paragraphs.

_____. "Events in the World of Music." March 26,
1944, Section 2:4.
Brief article of plans to take a portable production
of THE OLD MAID to Army camps. The cast,
pianist and director are listed. Two paragraphs.

_____. "Miss O'Malley Sings Menotti Opera Role."
October 10, 1948, 68.
Review at the City Center. Australian Muriel
O'Malley makes her City Center debut as Miss
Todd. She is a success both in acting and vocal-
ism. See also AMELIA.

_____. "New Radio Opera of Menotti Given." April 23,
1939, Section 3:6.

Review of the world premiere radio broadcast from
Radio City April 22. It is a new experience with
sound triumphant over sight. The English libretto
is served well with good diction and "fresh voices."
One hour is the length. THE OLD MAID is a success; Menotti handles the conversational situations
facilely. But there is ample expansive song such
as Miss Todd's solo and the passage for Bob "I
Must Wander Again." In contrast, there are gay
dance pieces and a fugue and scherzo for the
jewelry theft. It illustrates anew Menotti's inven-
tiveness. The cast sets a high standard. Alberto
Erede conducts and Richard Leonard is the production director. Seven paragraphs.

_____. "Round the Studios." April 2, 1939, Section 10:
12.

Article discussing the world premiere radio per-
formance. It would originate from WJZ at Radio
City. It is a "satirical farce." Singers will be
Robert Weede (Bob), Lydia Sommers (Miss Todd),
Margaret Daum (Metita) and Willa Stewart (Miss
Pinkerton). The NBC Symphony is to be conducted
by Alberto Erede. The last paragraph states in
error AMELIA was also written for radio.

_____. "Two Menotti Operas Given." September 28,
1952, 79.

Short review at the New York City Opera. Laurel
Hurley is a success in her first Laetita. See also
AMAHL.

_____. "Two Menotti Operas Heard." October 17, 1949,
19.

Brief notice at the City Center. Marie Powers is
Miss Todd. See also THE MEDIUM.

_____. "Two Operatic Novelties." February 12, 1941,
26.

Brief article about the first stage performance at
Philadelphia's Academy of Music performed by the
Philadelphia Opera Company. It is an amusing
success in a revised version.

THE SAINT OF BLEECKER STREET

_____. Atkinson, Brooks. January 2, 1955, Section 2:1.
Very perceptive review by a famed drama critic.
Atkinson concedes Menotti is a versatile man of the
theater. He finds the characters "inarticulate."
The literary style is "flat." Nevertheless, he ad-
mires the music and praises the performance.
Over a column.

_____. "Critics' Choice to Shostakovich." January 11,
1955, 19.
THE SAINT wins the New York Music Critics
Circle award for the best opera of 1954 on the
first ballot. Photo of Menotti.

_____. Doty, Robert C. "Menotti's 'Saint' Given at
Spoleto." July 8, 1968, 47.
Review of the Spoleto production, its first performance in Italy for thirteen years. Again the
public gives it a warm reception, but critics are
cooler. Menotti is quoted about the Milan public
loving THE SAINT but not the critics, some of
whom booed. Anna Maria Miranda is Annina,
Franco Bonisolli her brother and Gloria Lane "his
doxie." At the end there is an ovation for conductor Thomas Schippers and the Belgrade Philhar-
monic Orchestra. Critics have doubts about the
music. A quote from Mario Rinaldi's review in
Rome's Il Messaggero. THE SAINT is the first
Menotti opera presented at Spoleto. Eight short
paragraphs.

_____. Gould, Jack. "Television: A Saint and a Sinner."
January 19, 1956, 35.
Article about THE SAINT on "The Toast of the
Town" program on CBS Television. An excerpt
from Act II is given. Gould says the wedding reception scene comes across well on the screen.
He notes the television medium, camera close-ups,
e.g., seems fitted to Menotti's style. The singers
are David Poleri, Gloria Lane and Virginia Copeland. Four paragraphs.

_____. Grutzner, Charles. "Pulitzer Winners: 'Fable'
and 'Cat on Hot Tin Roof.'" May 3, 1955, 28.
Article. THE SAINT wins the Pulitzer Prize for

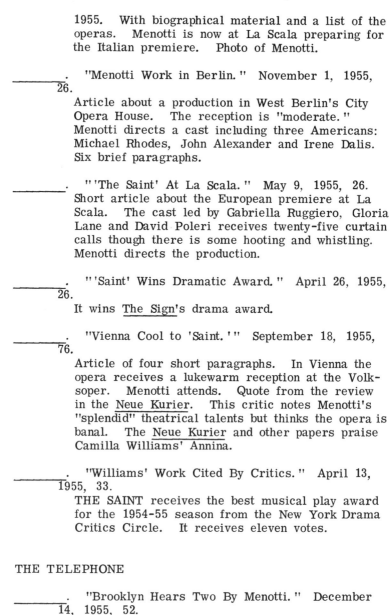

1955. With biographical material and a list of the operas. Menotti is now at La Scala preparing for the Italian premiere. Photo of Menotti.

_____. "Menotti Work in Berlin." November 1, 1955, 26.
Article about a production in West Berlin's City Opera House. The reception is "moderate." Menotti directs a cast including three Americans: Michael Rhodes, John Alexander and Irene Dalis. Six brief paragraphs.

_____. "'The Saint' At La Scala." May 9, 1955, 26.
Short article about the European premiere at La Scala. The cast led by Gabriella Ruggiero, Gloria Lane and David Poleri receives twenty-five curtain calls though there is some hooting and whistling. Menotti directs the production.

_____. "'Saint' Wins Dramatic Award." April 26, 1955, 26.
It wins The Sign's drama award.

_____. "Vienna Cool to 'Saint.'" September 18, 1955, 76.
Article of four short paragraphs. In Vienna the opera receives a lukewarm reception at the Volksoper. Menotti attends. Quote from the review in the Neue Kurier. This critic notes Menotti's "splendid" theatrical talents but thinks the opera is banal. The Neue Kurier and other papers praise Camilla Williams' Annina.

_____. "Williams' Work Cited By Critics." April 13, 1955, 33.
THE SAINT receives the best musical play award for the 1954-55 season from the New York Drama Critics Circle. It receives eleven votes.

THE TELEPHONE

_____. "Brooklyn Hears Two By Menotti." December 14, 1955, 52.
Brief review at the Brooklyn Academy of Music. The writer is not impressed with the shorter work. Its best moments are when Menotti's music domi-

nates the gags. The singers are Nadja Witkowska
and David Aiken. See also THE MEDIUM.

_____. Downes, Olin. "Opera by Menotti Has Its Pre-
miere. " February 19, 1947, 32.
Review of the world premiere of THE TELEPHONE
at the Heckscher Theatre. Downes views the short
opera buffa as a happy result, showing the composer's ability to write both melody and wit for a
practical theatre. Downes skillfully analyzes the
vocal music--the lady's types of aria, a "take-off"
of a Bellini duet and so forth. THE TELEPHONE
may be the shortest opera buffa of all. Plot summary. Three paragraphs. See also THE MEDIUM.

_____. "Menotti Operas in Unusual Show. " July 20,
1950, 22.
Review at the Arena "in the round. " Edith Gordon
is not adequate for her role. Paul King is more
effective as Ben. See also THE MEDIUM.

_____. Shanley, J. P. "By Popular Demand. " January
2, 1949, Section 2:3.
Article about the success of THE TELEPHONE and
THE MEDIUM in the United States and abroad.
Sixteen paragraphs. See also THE MEDIUM.

_____. "Two One-Act Operas Given. " November 21,
1955, 23.
Brief notice of a performance by the Empire Opera
Company in Carnegie Recital Hall. The singers
are Veli Slava and Fred Patrick.

THE UNICORN, THE GORGON AND THE MANTICORE

_____. Martin, John. "Menotti's 'Fable' Danced at Cen-
ter. " January 16, 1957, 36.
Review of THE UNICORN danced by the New York
City Ballet at the City Center. Martin thinks it is
more at home in a chamber music festival than on
stage. Here the music and the action and the
words work against each other. A "slow exposition" is followed by a situation repeated three times.
John Butler does the best possible with his choreography but despite its "cleverness" it cannot save
the production. The dancers perform excellently

and the setting is beautiful. Its interest is for only
a select audience. Eight paragraphs.

_____. Taubman, Howard. "Music: Opera By Menotti. "
October 22, 1956, 25.
Review of the world premiere at the Library of
Congress. Menotti goes back to the seventeenth
century to Monteverdi's madrigals. The dying
Poet's words are quoted. Taubman calls it an
"attractive fable. " To reverse a Menotti trend,
there is no "dramatic intensity. " Menotti's music
evokes another era with its madrigal forms. Plot
summary. Nine paragraphs. Photo of Menotti.

VII. GENERAL NEWSPAPER ARTICLES

New York Times. February 9, 1941, Section 9:3.
Left profile photo of Menotti before THE OLD MAID
is presented in Philadelphia.

_____. February 15, 1942, Section 8:7.
Profile photograph of the composer before THE
ISLAND GOD premiere.

_____. February 2, 1947, Section 2:9.
Left profile photo of Menotti before the premiere
of THE TELEPHONE.

_____. June 10, 1947, 38.
Photo of Menotti. The bill of THE TELEPHONE
and THE MEDIUM is extended at the Barrymore.

_____. May 29, 1966, Section 2:11.
Photo of the composer accompanying the article by
Howard Klein, "Menotti At War With Menotti."

_____. "Bertrand Russell, Menotti and Colette Named
Honorary Members of Arts Group." May 7, 1953, 10.
Menotti is named an honorary associate of The
National Institute of Arts and Letters. Photo of
Menotti.

_____. Downes, Olin. "Writer of Opera." March 2,
1947, Section 2:9.
Biographical article. THE TELEPHONE illustrates
Menotti's versatility as a composer and his practical sense of the stage. The props for it are very
few. The vocal parts are flexible for an aspiring
soprano or an accomplished baritone. L'Amour a
Trois, the subtitle, is a jest that has brought him
income. Downes then reviews the career. He
says THE ISLAND GOD failed because its libretto
was too symbolic and untheatrical. Menotti turns

177

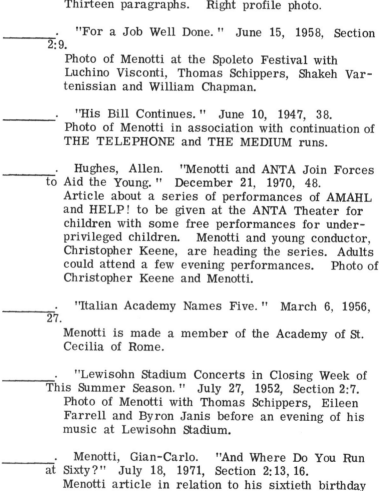

next to chamber operas. THE MEDIUM shows a
skill for the sensational. Whether THE MEDIUM
is "characteristic Menotti" is not resolved. Regardless, it functions admirably and should have an
effect on American opera. His Italian spirit stems
in part from La Scala and the Italian theatre. But
his creations are in "native lyric theatre, " good
entertainment that is practical for small performing
areas. His solid dramatic expression should ex-
pedite the growth of smaller American opera houses.
Thirteen paragraphs. Right profile photo.

_____. "For a Job Well Done. " June 15, 1958, Section
    2:9.
Photo of Menotti at the Spoleto Festival with
Luchino Visconti, Thomas Schippers, Shakeh Var-
tenissian and William Chapman.

_____. "His Bill Continues. " June 10, 1947, 38.
Photo of Menotti in association with continuation of
THE TELEPHONE and THE MEDIUM runs.

_____. Hughes, Allen. "Menotti and ANTA Join Forces
    to Aid the Young. " December 21, 1970, 48.
Article about a series of performances of AMAHL
and HELP! to be given at the ANTA Theater for
children with some free performances for under-
privileged children. Menotti and young conductor,
Christopher Keene, are heading the series. Adults
could attend a few evening performances. Photo of
Christopher Keene and Menotti.

_____. "Italian Academy Names Five. " March 6, 1956,
    27.
Menotti is made a member of the Academy of St.
Cecilia of Rome.

_____. "Lewisohn Stadium Concerts in Closing Week of
    This Summer Season. " July 27, 1952, Section 2:7.
Photo of Menotti with Thomas Schippers, Eileen
Farrell and Byron Janis before an evening of his
music at Lewisohn Stadium.

_____. Menotti, Gian-Carlo. "And Where Do You Run
    at Sixty?" July 18, 1971, Section 2:13, 16.
Menotti article in relation to his sixtieth birthday
on July 7. At age 60, there is the problem of

what direction the older artist should take. He had
not taken the word "success" to heart. After all,
look at the "damning" of his work by critics.
MARIA and AMAHL illustrate dramatic changes in
taste. He does not take his prizes too "seriously."
In stage direction he sees too much that is poor
although there are certain productions (six mentioned) that have taught him fine points. "Old, fat
opera singers" and those who are more concerned
with their high notes than the drama are dangerous
to opera's future as theater. His disillusionment
of never having his own opera company to train
young artists is small compared to his feelings
about his creations. The problem of parlar can-
tando he feels has not been solved. He admits a
great "torment" in not doing better with the "elu-
sive essence of melody, " for it has tremendous
moving powers in the theater. The letters from
children about AMAHL move him. Three letters
are quoted. With great pleasure he recalls THE
CONSUL in Israel, THE MEDIUM in Paris and interpretations by Marie Powers, Patricia Neway,
Chet Allen and Richard Cross. The Spoleto Festival has answered a great need for him. In the
final paragraph he indicates an indifference to
opera's future course. He has always found help
and understanding in his work when he needed it.
Large photo of Menotti on his sixtieth birthday.

_____. Menotti, Gian-Carlo. "If the Emperor's Naked,
A Child Will Know. " December 21, 1969, Section 2:
19.
    Menotti article about children as an audience.
    AMAHL is for children of his generation. HELP!
    is for the contemporary child. Six paragraphs.
    Photos: Invading Globolinks from the City Center
    production and of Menotti.

_____. "Missionary Author. " March 6, 1955, Section
2:1.
    Article about the new audience Menotti wants to
    attract. Broadway has a "ready-made audience" of
    large size that is much smaller for opera. Menotti
    believes a willingness to merely present new operas
    to the already existent audience can be fatal to it.
    He believes the artist should address himself to
    "man as he is ideally conceived" without trying to

satisfy any majority. The crisis now is that too
many artists are addressing a small, select audience. Menotti is interested in those who have never
seen an opera. But too many who agree with this
stance want to "oversimplify" standards. Menotti
claims he has done the opposite in THE MEDIUM
and THE CONSUL. In THE SAINT he has violated
commercial theatre taboos. This work calls for
four completely different settings. The orchestra
is larger than usual, fifty-six members. Menotti
has not provided a "pat solution" for its conclusion. He is "astonished" that the critics would
comment on the unresolved issues of THE SAINT.
Because he has broken the rules, THE SAINT's box
office problems do not surprise him. To Menotti
the importance of a "new convert" far outweighs
the reaction of the "habitues." Twelve paragraphs.

_____. "No Compromise on Art." January 16, 1957, 36.
Biographical article on the same day of UNICORN
review at the City Center. One paragraph has
several quotes on Menotti's ideals for art. One of
his central beliefs is that art should not be done
for money, that its standards should not be com-
promised for profit. Fourteen paragraphs. Photo
of Menotti at work on stage.

_____. "Parmenter, Ross. "World of Music: Lyric Ex-
plosion." November 26, 1959, Section 2:9.
Frank Merkling, editor of Opera News, says
Menotti is partly responsible for the new groups
performing operas and for the greater popularity
of modern operas. One paragraph.

_____. Taubman, Howard. "Director Resigns City Center
Post." January 28, 1955, 15.
Article about Lincoln Kirstein's resignation as
managing director of the City Center. Kirstein
had asked Menotti to be artistic director of the
opera company. THE SAINT had been commissioned under a Rockefeller Foundation grant.
Kirstein attempted to have THE SAINT premiered
at the City Center.

_____. Taubman, Howard. "Roving Troupe in West Adds
a Flair to Opera." March 1, 1969, 20.
References to Western Opera Theater performances

of a double bill of THE OLD MAID and THE
MEDIUM starting in January, 1967.   Photo of
Menotti.

NAME INDEX

Page numbers underlined refer to illustrations or photographs. Operas by other composers and other works are indexed although the author's name may not be in the text.

Aarden, Mimi 105
Ackart, Robert 111
Adler, Peter Herman 21, 161
Afeyan, B. 64
Aiken, David 20, 46, 59, 126, 145
Alberghetti, Anna Maria 89, 93, 94, 164
Alexander, John 158, 174
Alfano, Franco 121
Algermissen, Virginia vi
Allen, Chet 20, 26, 37, 42, 44, 46, 47, 126, 138-139, 142, 163, 179
Amadini, Maria 20
Anday, Rosette 91
Andersen, Christa 55
Apel, Willi 25
Aprahamian, Felix xv, 27, 50-51
Ardoin, John 51, 68, 73
Armistead, Horace 30, 53, 111, 149, 162
Armond, Raymond 49
Arutiunian, A. 64
Atkins, Norman 150
Atkinson, Brooks 147, 158, 162-163, 173
Aulicino, Armand 111
Ayars, Ann 163, 169

Backrass, Hannelore 105
Bacquier, Gabriel 78, 81
Bagar, Robert 26

Baisley, Helen 164
Baker, Margaret 21
Baker, Theodore 25
Balaban, Emanuel 21, 163
Baldini, G. 51
Barber, Samuel 24, 32
Barichella, Monique 81-82
Barlow, L. M. 72
Barnes, Clive 87
Baro, Gene 117, 161-162
Barraud, Henry 51
Barrett, Constance vi
Barzin, Leon 165
Batic, Polly 36
Bauch, J. N. 40
Bauer, Leda 89
Bauer, Marion 35
Baum, Vicki 121
Bayliss, Stanley 51
Beattie, Herbert 147
Beaurepaire, Andre 80, 156
Begou, Rene 55
Belasco, David 104
Bell, Eleanor 66
Bellingardi, Luigi 40, 46, 68
Bellini, Vincenzo 175
Bender, William 96
Benjamin, Arthur 51, 58
Berg, Alban 50, 115, 122, 153
Berman, Eugene 26, 41, 44-45, 46-47, 139-140
Bernard, Robert 25
Bernheimer, Martin 75

Bernstein, Bob 82
Beyer, William 90, 109
Biancolli, Louis 26
Bible, Frances 167
Bing, Sir Rudolf 33, 81,
    158
Bishop, Adelaide 169
Bizet, Georges 49
Blanc, Ernest 80
Blegen, Judith 21, 153,
    154
Blitzstein, Marc 101, 151
Blom, Eric
Bloomfield, T. 40, 68
Bloys, Marcel 92
Blum, David 26
Boettcher, Else 61
Boito, Arrigo 109
Boll, Andre 24
Bonaccorsi, Alfredo 26
Bonazzi, Elaine 74
Bonisolli, Franco 173
Bonvicini, Renzo 117
Borgonovo, Luigi 144
Borkh, Inge 61, 149
Bosch, Hieronymus 41,
    138
Boulez, Pierre 130
Bourgeois, J. 75
Bowen, Jean 75
Bower, Beverly 144
Brahms, Caryl 51, 63
Brahms, Johannes 119
Brando, Marlon 108
Bremini, Ireneo 101
Breuer, Robert 73, 75
Bridge, Walter 117
Briegk, Ralph 114
Briggs, John 26, 117-118,
    142, 163, 169
Brindle, Reginald 48, 52
Briner, A. 82
Britten, Benjamin 53, 62,
    66, 75, 88, 94, 112,
    152, 167
Brockway, Wallace 26
Bronhill, June 111

Brown, John Mason xv, 52,
    90, 109, 148
Browning, Kirk 139, 161
Browning, Robert 152
Brownlee, John 143
Brozen, Michael 75
Bruno, Joanna 96-98, 168
Bruyr, Jose 118
Bull, Storm 26
Bullard, Gene 148
Busoni, Ferruccio 122
Butler, Henry 24, 118
Butler, John 113, 115-116,
    175

Cairns, David 87
Calvin, Tony 95
Campi, Enrico 20, 142
Cantelmo, Ugo 144
Capderou, Janine 49, 92
Carlson, Claudine 21
Caron, Michel 49
Carosio, Margherita 4
Carroll, Joan 111, 163
Carron, Elisabeth 147
Carson, Elizabeth 170
Carter, John 155
Cartier, Rudolf 107
Casmus, Mary Irene xv-
    xvi, 22
Cassel, Walter 126
Castiglioni, V. 82
Castle, Peggy 95
Chamlee, Mario 143
Chapman, William 21, 150,
    158, 178
Charpentier, Gustave 93
Chase, Gilbert 27, 121
Chedorge, A. 82
Chiesa, Mary 109
Chmashkian, M. 64
Chookasian, Lili 21, 33,
    66-67, 75, 94, 132, 156-
    157, 166
Chotzinoff, Samuel 21, 118-
    119, 131, 139
Churchill, Sir Winston 162

Cimarosa, Domenico 77
Clarendon see Gavoty, Bernard
Clatworthy, David 139, 148
Clements, Joy 167
Clurman, Harold 52, 107
Cocteau, Jean 33
Cole, Dorothy 65
Cole, Sharon 116
Coleman, Emily 82
Coleman, Leo 26, 32, 37, 89, 93-94, 127, 164-165, 167
Collaer, Paul 27
Colombo, Franco 156
Coltellaci, G. 28
Cooper, June 152
Cooper, Martin 27, 90, 109
Copeland, Virginia 34, 108, 173
Copland, Aaron 32, 121
Cortesi, Arnaldo 145-146
Cotlow, Marilyn 21, 110-111, 112, 119, 135
Cowell, Henry 41, 54
Cowles, Chandler 53, 101, 119, 150-151, 166
Crader, Jeannine 56
Craig, Mary 90-91, 110
Cross, Milton 27
Cross, Richard 4-5, 20-21, 35, 45, 66, 82-83, 84-85, 118, 126, 140, 152, 158-159, 160-161, 179
Crowther, Bosley 163-164
Cunningham, Davis 34

d'Albert, Eugene Francis Charles 58
Dalis, Irene 174
Dalton, Wesley 155
Dame, Beverly 21
Damon, Oskar 145
Daniel, Ralph T. 25
Danjou, Jacqueline 92
Dannenberg, Peter 68

Danzus, Domenico 54
Darack, Arthur 54
Darlington, W. A. 114
Darrell, Peter 113
d'Attili, Maria 109
Daum, Margaret 49, 171-172
Davidson, Joy 65
Deakin, Audrey 95
Dean, Leigh 22
Debussy, Claude 115
Deke, R. F. xiv, 91
Delannoy, Marcel 24, 39
Delvaux, Lucienne 92
Demarquez, Suzanne 91
Depraz, Xavier 81
Derr, Emily 21
De Vries, Louise 54
Diamond, David 99
Diaz, Justino 67
Dickson, Muriel 20, 143
DiGerlando, Maria 126
Dillon, Irwin 143
Djilas, Milovan 145
Donizetti, Gaetano 78, 157
Doty, Robert 173
Dowling, Denis 34, 111
Downes, Edward 164, 170
Downes, Olin 90, 107, 109, 138-139, 143, 146-147, 155, 164-165, 170, 175, 177-178
Dragadze, Peter 83
Dresse, Francis 85
DuChamp, Marc 93, 122
DuCreux, Louis 130
Dumesnil, Rene 24, 75
Dunlap, Orrin E., Jr. 170-171
Dunlop, Lionel 101-102
Dunning, Edwin 167
Duparc, Henri 29
Duval, Franca 21, 35, 82-83, 84-85, 118, 126, 158-159, 160-161
Duvoisin, Roger 22
Dwyer, Terence 28

Eaton, Quaintance 28, 41-42, 99
Eckertsen, Dean 119
Edwards, Sydney 119-120
Elias, Rosalind 66, 152
Ellsworth, Ray 120
Engel, Lehman 20, 150
Engen, Keith 49
Englander, Roger 51, 150
Erede, Alberto 172
Ericson, Raymond 91, 147
Erwin, Richard 114
Evans, Beverly 147
Evett, Robert 83, 112, 120
Ewen, David 29
Eyer, Ronald 83

Farrell, Eileen 155, 178
Faull, Ellen 127, 135, 154, 170
Favors, Aaron 42
Fellini, Federico 122
Felton, James 66, 91
Fiechtner, Helmut 102
Figueroa, Tomas vi
Fioroni, Giovanna 65, 88
Fitzgerald, Gerald 75
Flagello, Ezio 33, 76, 156-157
Flanner, Janet 33
Floyd, Carlisle 132
Franci, Carlo 88
Franke, Paul 76
Frankenstein, Alfred 55
Franklin, Benno 30
Fredericks, Richard 150
Fredman, Myer 113
Freeman, John 96-97
Frost, Frances 22

Gaetani, Lorenzo 88
Gainey, Andrew 169
Galiano, Joseph 139
Gambetta, Rosario 83
Gance, Abel 93
Garde, Carlos 55
Gardino, Jolanda 54

Gavoty, Bernard 33, 75
Gaynes, George 150
Gedda, Nicolai 33, 156-157
Geitel, Klaus 42, 68, 102
Gelb, Arthur 158
George, Russell 59
George, Zelma 94-95, 96, 162, 168
Georgi, Yvonne 114-115, 151
Georgiou, Vilma 151
Gershwin, George 57, 102
Gesualdo, Don Carlo 130
Gilbert, William Schwenck 157
Giovaninetti, Reynald 82
Glaser, Milton 22
Glock, William 112
Goldovsky, Boris 29
Golea, Antoine 55, 76, 102
Goodman, John 91
Gordon, Edith 112, 175
Gordon, Norman 20, 155
Goth, Gisella Selden 102
Gould, Jack 148, 173
Goury, Jean 55
Graaf, Anneke van der 112
Graf, Herbert 30, 102
Graf, Max 91, 102
Greene, Harriet 143
Greenspon, Muriel 91-92, 95-96
Grimax, Daniele 85
Grossman, Herbert 20, 45, 161
Groth, Howard 121
Grout, Donald Jay 30
Grutzner, Charles 173-174
Guelfi, Piero 54
Guglielmi, Edoardo 88

Hagelstange, Rudolf 114
Haggin, B. H. 55, 73
Halasz, Laszlo 144
Halevy, Jacques Francois 78
Hallstein, Ingeborg 49-50
Hamburger, Philip 42
Hamm, Charles 30

Hammid, Sasha 165
Handt, Herbert 21, 35, 82, 84, 88
Hannon, Jean 89
Harewood, Earl of 31
Harrison, F. A. 39, 76
Harrison, Jay 107, 116
Haskins, Virginia 163
Hasslo, Hugo 62
Hayes, Richard 103
Hecht, Joshua 56
Hell, Henri 56
Heller, E. 110
Helm E. 76
Henahan, Donal 139, 152
Henze, Hans Werner 81
Herbe, Michele 55
Herbillon, Jacques 49, 92
Herman, Robert 33
Herzfeld, Friedrich 30
Hijman, Julius 43, 121
Hindemith, Paul 62, 122
Hinkson, Mary 45
Hinton, James Jr. 34, 48
Hirsch, Georges 79, 129
Hirsch, Nicole 121-122
Hoklen, Randall LeConte, Jr., 22-23
Holde, Arthur 43, 103
Holecek, Heinz 99
Hollander, Hans 122
Hollreiser, Heinrich 102
Holmes, Eugene 96-98, 167
Holthaus, Gerard 54
Honolka, Kurt 19
Hopple, Mary 171
Horan, Robert 24
Howard, John Taskar 30
Howe, Richard 91-92, 110
Hughes, Allen 139, 178
Hugo, Victor 127
Hurley, Laurel 172
Hyde, Anne 113

Ionesco, Eugene 24

Jacobs, Arthur 30, 56, 67, 77, 92
Jacques, Josette 55
Jamroz, Krystyna 56
Janacek, Leos 122
Janis, Byron 178
Jappe, Madeleine vi
Jaray, Hans 99
Jennings, Jerry 42
Joachim, Heinz 43, 56, 69
Jobin, Raoul 155
Johnson, David 84
Johnson, Harriet 37
Johnson, Louis 116
Jolly, Cynthia 34, 48
Jolly, Naomi vi
Jongeyans, George 53
Jooss, Kurt 168
Jordan, Kirk 141-142
Jurik, M. 56

Kaczynski, Tadeusz 56
Kafka, Franz 55
Kanski, Jozef 56, 123
Kantor, David 166
Kastendieck, Miles 57, 168
Katanian, A. 64
Katims, Milton 118
Kaufman, Wolfe 77
Kaufmann, Helen (Loeb) 31
Kay, Norman 123
Kayan, Orrin 116
Keene, Christopher 139, 168, 178
Keller, Evelyn 21, 26, 32, 37, 90
Kelley, Norman 52, 59, 148, 151, 158
Kemp, Robert 24
Kerman, Joseph 31
Kerr, Walter 107
Kessler, Hansi 67, 103
Khrennikov, Tikhon 38
King, Martha 20, 45, 140
King, Paul 109, 175
Kirstein, Lincoln 43, 57, 61, 103-104, 180

Klein, Howard 84, 148,
  162, 177
Klein, R. 84
Knapp, J. Merrill 31
Kobart, Ruth 83-84, 156
Kochnitzky, Leon 19, 22
Koegler, Horst 104
Kohn, Karl Christian 50
Kohrs, Karl 27
Kolodin, Irving x, 31, 44,
  57, 73, 84, 92, 97, 104,
  110, 124
Kombrink, Ilona 161
Konya, Sandor 105
Kova, Marija 155
Krause, Horst 114
Krebs, Beatrice 170
Kremer, Martin 105
Kreste, Mary 169
Krohn, Emmylou 42
Krokover, Rosalyn 113
Krutch, Joseph Wood 58,
  92, 110
Kubly, Herbert 124
Kuhlman, Rosemary 20,
  26, 37, 40, 45-46, 47,
  137, 139, 141-142, 146
Kuntzsch, Matthias 69
Kupferberg, Herbert 69
Kursova, Marketa 67
Kwartin, Paul 110-111,
  112, 119

LaMarchina, Robert 75,
  78, 158, 166
Landowski, Marcel 24, 75
Lane, Gloria 21, 34, 52,
  59, 64, 105-106, 107-
  108, 128, 129, 147, 150-
  151, 173-174
Lang, Paul Henry 31
Lansdale, Nelson 124
Lardner, John 92, 110
Las, Genia 21
LaSelva, Vincent 148
Lazzarini, Adriana 82
Leinsdorf, Erich 21, 67, 152

Lenoir, Jean-Pierre 156
Leonard, Richard 172
Leoncavallo, Ruggiero 125
Lesur, Daniel 24
Leue, Gregor 114
Levine, Joseph 113
Levinger, Henry 44, 58, 105
Lieberman, Rolf 68
Lieberson, Goddard 21
Liebling, Leonard 48
Lillich, Meredith xv, 124-125
Lishner, Leon 20-21, 26, 52,
  59-60, 64, 135, 145, 148
Lloyd, Norman 32
Lockspeiser, Edward 58
London, George 21, 33, 66-
  67, 74-77, 79-80, 152, 156
Louchheim, Aline B. 139
Loveland, Kenneth 88
Lowendahl, Walter 166
Ludgin, Chester 65, 148
Luten, C. J. 67
Lyons, James 21

McCollum, John 20, 45
McDonald, Dennis 44, 99
Maciejewski, B. M. 88
McIntyre, Donald 87, 162
McIver, Bill 40, 47, 137,
  140
MacKayle, Donald 140
McKerrow, Rita 95
McKinley, Andrew 20, 46,
  146
McLaughlin, Kathleen 149
McLiesh, Fleming 4, 20,
  155
MacNeil, Cornell 25, 52,
  57
MacNeil, Dorothy 163, 167
MacPherson, George 95
McSpadden, J. Walker 32
MacWatters, Virginia 100,
  170
Mahlke, E. 105
Maione, Rino 125-126
Malipiero, Riccardo 105

Maliponte, Adriana 156
Mangin, Noel 42
Mannes, Marya 105
Mari, Pierrette 49, 92
Marks, Marcia 44, 70
Marlo, Maria 53, 59, 148,
    150-151
Marsh, Calvin 158
Martin, George 32
Martin, John 175
Martin, Thomas P. 169
Marx, Henry 44, 58, 99
Mascagni, Pietro 29, 79,
    125
Massenet, Jules 49, 108
Mastice, Catherine 21
Mathis, Edith 69, 71-72
Mattfeld, Julius 32
Matthews, Thomas 32
Matz, Mary Jane 32
Mayer, Margery 142
Mayer, Martin 78
Mayer, Tony 85
Mayer, William 33
Mazzoni, E. 20
Mead, George 18, 20
Mellen, Constance 85, 113-
    114
Mellers, Wilfrid 126
Meloni, Claude 55
Menotti, Amalita 32, 133
Menotti, Gian Carlo (articles
    and excerpts) 29-32, 39,
    93, 123, 126-128, 156,
    165-166, 178-179
Menotti, Gian Carlo (photo-
    graphs and illustrations)
    21, 24-27, 29-34, 36,
    42, 46, 48-49, 53, 60,
    66, 74, 81-83, 89, 91,
    93, 95, 100, 111-113,
    117-123, 125-128, 130-
    131, 133-135, 141, 143,
    152, 154-155, 161, 171,
    173-174, 176-181
Meredith, Morely 33, 75,
    77-78, 156-157

Merkling, Frank 33, 70, 180
Mesavage, Karen 49
Mesple, Mady 78, 81, 156
Mester, Jorge 21
Metcalf, William 170
Meyer, Kerstin 42
Meyer, Laverne 113
Meyerbeer, Giacomo 78
Meyerowitz, Jay 33
Miazza, Georges 55
Migenes, Julia 148
Mikadian, E. 64
Mikhailow, M. 64
Miller, Philip 45
Milnes, Sherrill 147
Mincer, Richard 141-142
Mintz, Donald 159
Miranda, Anna Maria 173
Misselwitz, Matthias 42
Mitgang, Herbert 166
Monachino, Frank 20, 46
Monette, LaVergne 148
Montagu, George 59
Monteverdi, Claudio 115, 167
Montgomery, Robert 141
Montresor, Beni 22, 75,
    78-79, 81, 157
Moore, Douglas 132
Moore, Frank Leslie 33
Moorefield, Olive 99
Morley, Ruth 161
Moser, Jans Joachim 34
Mousset, Edouard 85
Movshon, George 97
Moynagh, Joan Marie 87
Mozart, Wolfgang Amadeus 143
Muser, Susanne 105
Musitz, Susanne 113
Mussorgsky, Modest xiii,
    62, 102-103, 115, 118,
    129, 131
Muti, Lorenzo 82

Nagy, Robert 158
Neumann, Therese 104, 128
Neway, Patricia viii, 20-21,
    24-26, 35, 37, 51, 52-53,

Neway (cont.)
  57, 59-64, 82, 95, 111,
  118, 126, 129, 135, 145-
  151, 158, 161, 164, 179
Newman, Arthur 142
Nikolais, Alwin 68, 70, 154
Nono, Luigi 63
Nordlinger, Genson, Jr. 114

Ohnen, Frank 78
Olson, Carl 144
O'Malley, Muriel 171
Orlando 132
Osborne, Conrad 79, 106

Panerai, Rolando 20
Panizza, Ettore 37, 143-
  144, 155
Pannain, Guido 33
Parinaud, Andre 129
Parmenter, Ross 144, 149-
  150, 151-152, 157, 166, 180
Patak, L. 59
Patrick, Fred 175
Patrick, Julian 21, 45, 140
Patterson, Willis 20, 45, 140
Pauly, Reinhard 35
Peabody, George Foster 141
Peiper, Ethel 72-73
Peiper, Herbert 35
Peltz, Mary Ellis 86
Penderecki, Krzysztof 71,
  153
Perez, Jose 167
Perry, Douglas 139
Pestalozza, Luigi 59
Peters, Roberta 33, 74-
  78, 80, 156-157
Petrella, Clara 54, 82-83,
  146
Petri, Mario 82-83
Phelan, Frank 79, 96
Phelan, Kappo 60, 93, 111
Piazza, Marguerite 143
Pierson, Edward 139
Pincherle, Marc 79
Pinzauti, Leonardo 130

Pirandello, Luigi 48
Pizetti, Ildebrando 121
Plasson, Michel 92
Plussain, Michel 79
Poleri, David 21, 106, 126,
  173-174
Politzer, Heinz 60
Pollak, Anna 61
Pollock, M. 45
Pondeau, Monique de 93
Popper, Felix 144
Poretta, Frank 74
Potvin, Gilles 115
Poulenc, M. Francis 57,
  79, 109
Pound, Ezra 120
Povia, Charlotte 148-149
Powers, Marie 20-21, 24-
  26, 37, 52-53, 57, 60-
  61, 63, 89-91, 93-95,
  100, 118, 126-129, 135,
  145-146, 151, 161-163,
  164-165, 167, 170, 172, 179
Prandelli, Giacinto 20
Prawy, Marcel 36
Price, Leontyne 158
Price, Olwen 34
Prideaux, Tom 32, 74
Prieberg, Fred 36
Privez, G. 55
Prokofiev, Sergei 81, 118
Proust, Marcel 86
Puccini, Giacomo xiii, 29,
  35, 49, 58, 62-64, 69,
  77-78, 88, 97, 102, 107-
  108, 115, 118-119, 120,
  122, 124-125, 129, 131,
  134, 147, 153-155, 159,
  168
Puleo, Robert 139, 141

Raskin, Judith 73-74, 126
Ratti, Eugenia 126
Razboynikov, S. 111
Reardon, John 21, 73-74,
  87, 126, 144
Reed, Janet 113

Reich, Willi 67, 106
Reid, Charles 35
Reiner, Fritz vii, 119
Reinhardt, Max 107
Reisfeld, Bert 74
Remy, Odette 92
Resnik, Regina 21
Respighi, Ottorino 63
Reynolds, Anna 21
Reynolds, Michael 80
Rhodes, Michael 174
Rich, Alan 80, 97, 150
Rieck, Ursula 114
Riemann, Hugo 36
Rigault, Jean de 93-94
Rilliard, Abel 92
Rinaldi, Alberto 88
Rinaldi, Mario 115, 173
Rizzo, Francis 70, 131
Rodgers, Richard 157
Rogers, Harold 67
Rogier, Frank 21, 110, 135
Rohs, Martha 36
Romagnoli, Mary 46
Rosen, George 86
Rosenstock, Joseph 167
Rosenthal, Harold 34, 36
Rosenthal, Jean 53
Rosenwald, Hans 131
Rossini, Gioacchino 75,
    109, 119, 157
Rother, Artur 149
Rott, Adolf 91
Rouse, Jack 70
Roussel, Albert 63
Rubes, Jan 145
Rudel, Julius 144
Ruggiero, Gabriella 21,
    34, 105, 126, 128, 174
Ruppel, Karl Hans 36

Saal, Herbert 97-98
Sabin, Robert 29, 61, 80,
    94, 106
Sachs, Evelyn 148, 150
Sadowski, Andrzej 123
Sahl, Hans 61

Samartini, Pier Luigi 96
Sammarco, James 138
Samuel, Claude 75, 80,
    133-134
Sanborn, Pitts 37
Sandberg, Ingrid 62
Sanzogno, Nino 20, 48, 142,
    146
Sardou, Victorien 104
Sarfaty, Regina 148
Sargeant, Winthrop viii, x,
    xv, 24, 29, 38, 49, 56,
    62, 68, 74, 86, 89, 94,
    97-98, 107-108, 131-133
Sarnette, Eric 81
Sarocca, Suzanne 85
Sauguet, Henri 24
Saunders, Arlene 69, 71,
    154
Scalero, Rosario 119, 132
Scarlatti, Domenico 130
Schaefer, Theodore 115
Scharley, Denise 85, 93, 122
Schauensee, Max de 86
Scheuremann, Leona 167
Schippers, Thomas 20-22,
    65, 81, 94, 105, 137-
    138, 141, 144, 151, 155,
    157, 169, 173, 178
Schmidt-Garre, H. 50
Schneiders, Heinz-Ludwig
    70-71
Schoeffer, Nicolas 68, 70,
    154
Schoenberg, Arnold 122,
    130, 161
Scholes, Percy 36
Schonberg, Harold 70, 80,
    141, 150, 153-154, 156-
    157, 168-169
Schubert, Franz Peter 129-
    130
Schulz, Rudolf 114
Schuman, William 32, 118
Schweizer, G. 105
Scott, Marc 118, 163
Scott, Norman 76

Scribe, Augustin Eugene 104
Seelmann-Eggebert, Ulrich 108
Seltsam, William 37
Semkov, Jerzy 67
Serafin, Enzo 165
Severi, G. 86
Shakespeare, William 150
Shanet, Howard 46
Shanley, J. P. 166, 175
Shawe-Taylor, Desmond 62,
    94, 111
Shuard, Amy 34, 61
Signorelli, Maria 144
Silva, Roberto 144
Simard, Paulette 55
Simionato, Guilietta 47
Simon, Henry 37
Sinclair, Monica 95
Singer, Samuel 67
Slava, Veli 175
Sliwinski, Zdzistaw 123
Slonimsky, Nicholas 38,
    118
Smith, Carol 67
Smith, Cecil 50, 62-63,
    94-95, 100, 111
Smith, French Crawford 87
Smith, Oliver 168
Smith, Patrick 38, 71
Sommers, Lydia 172
Somogi, Judith 139
Soria, Dorle J. 81
Starling, William 26
Stein, Elliott 81
Stepanian, A. 64
Sternfeld, Frederick 100
Stewart, Willa 171-172
Stilwell, Richard 85
Stokowski, Leopold 47
Storrer, William 46
Stratas, Teresa 33, 76,
    156-158
Strauss, Richard 62, 115,
    118, 147
Stravinsky, Igor viii, 33,
    69, 112, 130
Stronglin, Theodore 158

Stuart, Charles xiv, 63
Sullivan, Arthur Seymour 157
Sullivan, Dan 141
Summers, Lydia 156
Sutcliffe, James Helme 47,
    71, 154
Swanson, Howard 118
Swenson, Swen 116
Szczepanska, Krystyna 56
Szemere, Laszlo 36

Taubman, Howard 134-135,
    142, 150-151, 159-161,
    167, 176, 180-181
Taylor, William 135
Ter-Arutaninga, Reuben 82,
    161
Terrasson, Rene 55
Terry, Walter 116
Ter-Simonyan, M. 64
Thar, David 49
Theyard, Harry 168
Thompson, Oscar 38
Thomson, Virgil 32, 38,
    57, 90
Todd, Arthur 135-136
Tooker, George 104
Torday, S. 47
Torkanowsky, Werner 148,
    150, 167
Toscanini, Arturo viii-ix,
    111, 134-135, 143
Tracey, Edmund 33
Treash, Leonard 49
Trebor, Emil 98
Trevin, J. C. 64
Tricoire, Robert xvi, 24
Trimble, Leslie 87
Triotschel, Elfride 105
Trommer, Wolfgang 114-
    115
Tucci, Gabriella 128
Turner, Claramae 91, 163
Tyers, John 169

Ubel, Ruth 81
Ulanov, Barry 64

Untermeyer, Louis 20

Vajda, Igor 65
Van Mantgem, Jan 54
Varnay, Astrid 155
Vartenissian, Shakeh 178
Vecchi, Orazio 113, 115
Velis, Andrea 76
Ven Frans van der 112
Venora, Lee 164, 169
Verdi, Giuseppe 109, 115,
   118, 121, 127, 143
Vigolo, Giorgio 24
Visconti, Luchino 178
Voketaitis, Arnold 148
Volbach, Walter 39
Voltaire 130
Votto, Antonino 144

Waas, Adolph 67
Wagner, K. 47, 71
Wagner, Richard 106, 130,
   157, 165
Wallerstein, Lothar 155
Warren, Leonard 155
Watmough, David 65
Watson, Corinne 23
Watson, Jack M. 39
Watts, Douglas 47, 65,
   100
Weaver, William 65, 95-
   96
Webern, Anton von 153
Wechsberg, Joseph 39
Weede, Robert 171-172
Weiler, A. H. 168
Weinstock, Herbert 26, 71-
   72, 98
Weiss, Bernard 114
Weisstein, Ulrich 39
Wennink, Michael 87-89,
   162
Wentworth, Richard 45
Werker, G. 112
Westermann, Gerhart von 39
Westrup, J. A. 39
Wettergren, Gertrud 62

Whallon, Evan 163
White, Robert 73-74
Whitebait, William 96
Wicherek, Antoni 123
Willauer, Marguerite 153
Williams, Camilla 102, 174
Williams, Nancy 139
Williams, Tennessee 120
Wilson, Charles 149
Winkler, Georg 18
Winters, Lawrence 45, 137
Witkowska, Najda 175
Wolansky, Raymond 69
Wolff, Beverly 74, 97-98,
   168
Wolf-Ferrari, Ermanno 29,
   37, 62, 111
Worbs, Hans Christoph 72
Workman, William 42, 69,
   71-72
Wyatt, Euphemia van Rens-
   salaer 48, 65-66, 96,
   108, 112
Wylie, Barbara vi

Yaghjian, Kurt 20, 140-141
Yarustovsky, Boris 136
Yeend, Frances 126
Young, Norman 170
Young, Percy 39

Zambrana, Margarita 65
Zanolli, S. 20
Zeani, Virginia 65
Zimbalist, Efrem Jr. 53,
   119, 151
Zoff, O. 108
Zolotow, Maurice 109, 151
Zytowski, C. B. 72